POEMS OF

René Char

POEMS OF
RENÉ CHAR

Translated and annotated by

MARY ANN CAWS and

JONATHAN GRIFFIN

Princeton University Press
Princeton, New Jersey

à Tina Jolas

M.A.C.   J.G.   R.C.

TABLE OF CONTENTS

x

xii

Top: René Char, 1973. (Photo: Lufti Özkök)
Bottom left: René Char. Les Busclats, 1975. (Photo: Peter Caws)
Bottom right: René Char. (Photo: Jacques Robert)

"Fête des arbres et du chasseur." Drawing in India ink. René Char, 1950. (Previously unpublished)

Cyprès que le chasseur blesse.

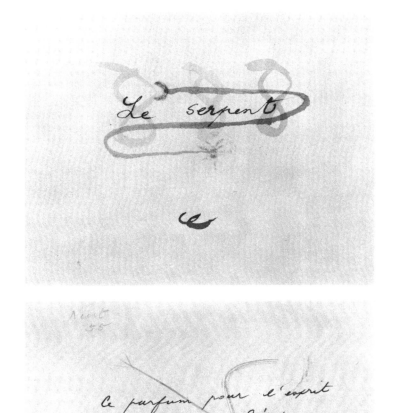

Top: Cover for the manuscript of the poem "Le Serpent." Drawing, wash, and india ink. René Char, 1955. (Previously unpublished)

Bottom: Verso of cover for the manuscript of the poem "Le Serpent." Ink and pastel. René Char, 1955. (Previously unpublished)

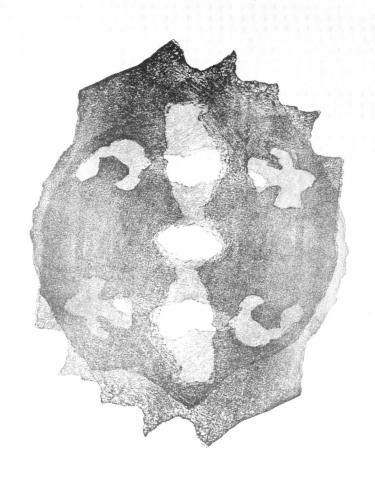

Pablo Picasso. Artist's proof of engraving for *Les Transparents*.
(Previously unpublished)

CHRONOLOGY

René Char

1907 Birth at L'Isle-sur-Sorgue, Vaucluse, in South of France.

1928 *Les Cloches sur le coeur* [René-Emile Char] (written between 1922-1926), Editions Le Rouge et Le Noir.

1929 *Arsenal*; Char sends copy to Eluard, who comes to L'Isle. Char meets with surrealist group in Paris.

1930 *Ralentir travaux* (in collaboration with Breton and Eluard), Editions surréalistes. *Artine*, Editions surréalistes.

1931 *L'Action de la justice est éteinte*, Editions surréalistes.

1934 *Le Marteau sans maître* (collected edition), Corti.

1935 Separation from surrealist group.

1937 *Placard pour un chemin des écoliers* (illustrated by Valentine Hugo), G.L.M.

1938 *Dehors la nuit est gouvernée*, G.L.M.

1940-1945 "Capitaine Alexandre" in the Resistance; regional head of a partisan group in the Alpes-de-Provence. In July 1944, ordered to Algiers on an advisory mission to the Supreme Allied Headquarters.

1945 *Seuls demeurent*, Gallimard.*

1946 *Feuillets d'Hypnos*, Gallimard. *Le Poème pulvérisé*, Editions Fontaine.

1948 *Fureur et mystère* (collected edition), Gallimard.*

1949 *Le Soleil des eaux* (illustrated by Braque). Librairie Matarasso.

1950 *Les Matinaux* (collected edition), Gallimard.*

1951 *A une sérénité crispée*, Gallimard.

Unless otherwise stated, place of publication is Paris.

* Indicates works included in one of the popular current editions (collection "Poésie/Gallimard")

1952 *La Paroi et la prairie*, G.L.M. *Le Rempart de brindilles* (illustrated by Wifredo Lam), Louis Broder.

1954 *A la santé du serpent* (illustrated by Miró), G.L.M.

1955 *Recherche de la base et du sommet*, followed by *Pauvreté et privilège* (collected edition [prose texts]), Gallimard.*

1956 *Les Compagnons dans le jardin* (illustrated by Zao Wou-Ki). Louis Broder.

1957 *Poèmes et prose choisis* (collected edition), Gallimard.

1960 *L'Inclémence lointaine* (illustrated by Vieira da Silva), Pierre Berès.

1962 *La Parole en archipel* (collected edition), Gallimard.*

1963 *Lettera amorosa* (illustrated by Braque), Gallimard.

1964 *Commune présence* (anthology), Gallimard.

1965 *Retour amont* (illustrated by Giacometti), G.L.M.

1967 *Trois coups sous les arbres, Théâtre saisonnier* (collected edition of theater), Gallimard. *Les Transparents* (illustrated by Picasso), Alès, P.A.B.

1968 *Dans la pluie giboyeuse*, Gallimard.

1971 *L'Effroi la joie* (illustrated by Sima), Jean Hugues. Exposition René Char at Fondation Maeght and Musée d'Art moderne de la Ville de Paris, *Catalogue-Anthologie*.

1972 *Le Nu perdu* (collected edition), Gallimard. *La Nuit talismanique* (illustrated by the poet), Geneva, Skira.

1975 *Le Monde de l'art n'est pas le monde du pardon* (texts on and for painters; illustrations by Klee, Kandinsky, Villeri, Braque, Matisse, Hugo, N. de Staël, Brauner, Fernandez, Grenier, Charbonnier, Miró, Lam, Reichek, Char, Picasso, Zao Wou-ki, Vieira da Silva, Giacometti, Szenes, Sima, Boyan, Pierre-André Bénoit; preface by Jacques Dupin), Maeght.

1975 *Aromates chasseurs*, Gallimard.

ACKNOWLEDGMENTS

Our grateful thanks for the permission to use the following texts: *"Vers quelle mer enragée,"* "Robustes météores," "A l'Horizon remarquable," "Bel édifice et les pressentiments," "Sosie," "Artine," "Poètes," "La Luxure," "Chaîne," "Vivante demain," "L'Eclaircie," "Migration," "Moulin premier" (extraits), and "Commune présence," from *Le Marteau sans maître,* © 1934, by Corti; "Compagnie de l'écolière," "Les Casseurs de cailloux," "Une Italienne de Corot," and "Remise," from *Dehors la nuit est gouvernée, précédé de Placard pour un chemin des écoliers,* © 1938, by G.L.M.; *"L'homme fuit l'asphyxie,"* "Envoûtement à la Renardière," "Le Loriot," "L'Absent," "L'Epi de cristal égrène dans les herbes sa moisson transparente," "Louis Curel de la Sorgue," "Ne s'entend pas," "Vivre avec de tels hommes," "Chant du refus," "Carte du 8 novembre," "Hommage et famine," "La Liberté," "Conduite," "Le Visage nuptial," "Evadné," "Post-scriptum," "Le Thor," "Pénombre," "Cette fumée qui nos portait," "Cur secessisti?," "Redonnez-leur," "Fastes," "Les Premiers instants," "Le Martinet," "La Sorgue," "Madeleine à la veilleuse," "Allégeance," *"Comment vivre sans inconnu devant soi,"* "Les Trois Soeurs," "Biens égaux," "J'Habite une douleur," "Louis Curel de la Sorgue," "Seuil," "L'Extravagant," and "Le Requin et la mouette," from *Fureur et mystère,* © 1948, by Gallimard; "Prière rogue," and "Avec Braque, peut-être, on s'était dit," from *Recherche de la base et du sommet,* © 1955, by Gallimard; *"Nous avons en nous sur notre versant tempéré,"* "Pyrénées," "Qu'il vive!," "Grège," "L'Amoureuse en secret," "Montagne déchirée," "L'Adolescent souffleté," "Recours au ruisseau," "Le Masque funèbre," "Les Lichens," "Joue et dors," "Les Inventeurs," "Homme-oiseau mort et bison mourant," "Les Cerfs noirs,"

"La Bête innommable," "Jeune cheval à la crinière vaporeuse," "Transir," "Le Taureau," "La Truite," "Le Serpent," "L'Alouette," "La Minutieuse," "L'Inoffensif," "Le Mortel partenaire," "Front de la rose," "Marmonnement," "Le Risque et le pendule," "Pour renouer," "Le Bois de l'Epte," "Victoire éclair," "La Chambre dans l'espace," "Rapport de marée," "Invitation," "La Bibliothèque est en feu," "Sur une nuit sans ornement," "Pour un Prométhée saxifrage," "Déclarer son nom," "Traverse," "La Faux relevée," "Contrevenir," "Allégresse," and "Fontis," from *Les Matinaux*, © 1950, and *La Parole en archipel*, © 1962, by Gallimard; *"Nous nous sentons complètement détachés,"* "Tracé sur le gouffre," "Chérir Thouzon," "Mirage des aiguilles," "Aux portes d'Aerea," "Devancier," "Venasque," "Les Parages d'Alsace," "Dansons aux Baronnies," "Possessions extérieures," "Faction du muet," "Yvonne," "Le Nu perdu," "Célébrer Giacometti," "Septentrion," "Lied du figuier," "Le Village vertical," "Le Jugement d'octobre," "Lenteur de l'avenir," "Le Banc d'ocre," "Lutteurs," "Déshérence," "Bout des solennités," "Le Gaucher," "L'Ouest derrière soi perdu," *"Où passer nos jours* à présent," "D'un même lien," "Tables de longévité," "Cotes," "Sortie," "Tradition du météore," "Jeu muet," "Rémanence," "Cours des argiles," "Dyne," "Bienvenue," "Permanent invisible," "Les Apparitions dédaignées," "Même si," "Aversions," "Bons voisins," and "Contre une maison sèche," from *Le Nu perdu*, © 1972, by Gallimard; "L'Anneau de la Licorne," "La Flamme sédentaire," "Don hanté," "Eprouvante simplicité," "Eclore en hiver," and "Sommeil aux Lupercales," ©, by René Char, from *La Nuit talismanique*, Skira, 1972; "Évadé d'archipel" and "Réception d'Orion," © by Gallimard, 1975.

All illustrations courtesy of René Char.

Thanks to Anthony Rudolf and the *Journal of Pierre Ménard* for permission to reprint the translations by Jonathan Griffin included there, and to *Twentieth Century Literature* for two translations by Mary Ann Caws.

PREFACES

In their diversity, the texts found in this volume represent various aspects of the work of René Char. In collaboration with the poet, we have selected prose and verse poems from the whole span of his work, stretching from 1927 to the present, including the shortest lyrics and the more solemn meditations. "The aspects of regimens alternate": there are no air-tight enclosures in his poetry, with the result that *Les Matinaux* offers its morning light to the more reserved contemplation of *La Nuit talismanique* and receives in return some of its stillness; *Le Marteau sans maître* serves as the dynamic source for, and the strange prediction of, *Fureur et mystère*, which, still maintaining its partial obscurity, confers on the first enigmatic collection a retrospective passion. A poetic faith endures: so the night, finally lit by a talisman, has an order of its own— *Dehors la nuit est gouvernée*—and a driving force, unremitting in its intensity, can be discerned always as leading in one direction, upland to a country more stark, the land of the *Nu perdu*, where the spiritually naked consciousness, bare of useless possessions, is absorbed, or then lost, within a space befitting it.

Of all Char's titles, the most appropriate to our presentation might be *Recherche de la base et du sommet*: for each individual reader could hope to find here both the foot and the peak of a poetic mountain. Every reading will choose its own profundity, its depth ("la base"), as well as its height ("le sommet"); we have chosen above all not to limit its possible trajectory or its scope.

Side by side with the dense and complex prose poems whose surface is marked by a particular intensity are to be found those texts constructed in what we might call lasting flashes, "des éclairs durables," where the intermittent illumination of a nonetheless enduring perception takes a brief and yet total form. A series of epic love poems and their corresponding but quieter poems of fidelity in spite of loss contrast with the singular and powerful descriptions of a figure with a sure gait whose "aggressive respiration" makes itself felt in his presence or his absence, through whose changing but coherent guises there persists the poet's unmistakable profile. The internal correspondence of the texts to one another finally triumphs over the external diversity. In this entire range, from the past and the contemplation of ancestral traces (as in the series of Lascaux poems) to Char's continuing concern with actual poetics ("La Bibliothèque est en feu" and *Sur la poésie*, extending from 1936-1974) the same moral commitment can be followed, dominant over the changing tone. The poet's voice echoes with memories now of Heraclitus, now of Shakespeare, or Hölderlin, Nietzsche, Rimbaud, Rilke, Melville, but the diverse strains do not interrupt it as the alterations of a visage do not affect the basic traits: the portrait remains constant.

The vast space gathered into this poetry is evident even in the titles already quoted. Yet, like the alchemical Work and the natural harvest against whose tapestries the poems are seen unfolding, the force of the whole is cyclical rather than dispersed, the effect integral rather than diffuse. Recurrent themes in their successive, sometimes intricate development are linked by a precise vocabulary and multiple images in echo: thus, for instance, the motif of the hunter whose prey is finally himself, "chasseur de soi,"[1] provides an *Arsenal* of weapons, powerful like the hammering action at once concrete and metaphorical—*Le Marteau sans maître*—for the poetic utterance said to fly forth like an arrow. At the same time the hunter motif joins the human to the animal world, where the wolf is man's equal and his double ("Let us remain—for our living and our dying—*with the wolves*"),[2]

[1] "Les trois soeurs," *Fureur et mystère*.

[2] The poet's statement on *Retour amont*, placed here as an introduction to *Le Nu perdu*.

since both are pursuing and pursued, and finally opens those realms to the mythological one, where a simple flower, "Orion's dart,"[3] leads us back to the single horn of a legendary animal alone in his constellation, as the unicorn's ring[4] leads once more, in a cyclical movement, to the hunter pursuing and, at last, caught.

The correspondence of the outer and inner landscapes is no less constant. The sparse formal contour of each individual text, often arduous, is balanced by the generous conviction of the only partly spoken interior legend created throughout the course of the entire work in its profusion of figures and imagery, set in an allusive scenery where the natural converges with the naturally mysterious. The spirit of Provence inhabits René Char as surely as he inhabits the region; a particular vegetation, a particular rocky aridity, and a particular luminosity befit the poet's own violent and yet illuminating presence, shifting in its response, and still of an unbending will: "We remain men for inclemency."[5] The difficulty of many of these poems matches that of this landscape, beyond which they extend, yet in which they endure, for the geographical determination is far from absolute, as the closed valley of the Vaucluse leads to a universe of great breadth.

This meeting between two regions of significance, the outer and the inner, is reflected by others: those between reader and poet, and, here, between the text and the translator, in whom—says René Char—the poem must necessarily remake itself, unceasingly. "There is the sense and the named, and the naming, and the mystery one might disturb by one's partisan judgement. . .":[6] in the light of the poet's words, we have tried to avoid the inflection of his path toward one private reading or another. Thus the translations are meant to cling as closely as is fitting to the original sense, whose expression in its ambiguities and deliberate difficulties they choose, whenever possible, not to resolve, whose intri-

[3] "Jeu muet," *Le Nu perdu.*
[4] "L'anneau de la Licorne," *La Nuit talismanique.*
[5] "Contrevenir," *La Parole en archipel.*
[6] Correspondence.

cacies of verbal echo and assonance they cannot often imitate. The poem in English should suffice in its own saying; if it seldom hopes to maintain exactly the same register, it can sometimes hope to discover an inner resonance not unfaithful. That is the goal of our translations.

A few examples may illustrate more effectively than can a general discourse some of the specific problems of translating René Char. Above all, the impulse toward figurative interpretation, of the sort we might permit ourselves in the translation of other poets, had on many occasions to be resisted, as this poet wills his literal and yet many-sided terms to remain literal; when concessions to one side or the other had to be made, they were habitually made in favor of the exigencies of the French original. This choice will be obvious and has not been regretted in the long run.

But it was a very long run. The struggle seemed never to be keenest where we might have expected, some of the simplest terms requiring the most frequently renewed effort. The case of some titles might be of interest: "L'Extravagant," because of its etymological breakdown into *extra* and *vagor* tempted us to a longer rendering, which seemed felicitous: "The Wanderer Outside." But there the literal sense of the extreme was lost, so that the more pleasing title had to be sacrificed for the plainer one: "The Extravagant One." For "J'habite une douleur" we initially gave "I Inhabit a Grief," simply through a preference for the beautiful word "grief" over the flatness of "pain." But it failed to convey the double moral and physical suffering; then, since "pain" was too awkward a final word, the order was modified to give "A Pain I Dwell In."

When, on the other hand, the literal could be included in the multiple, this choice was preferred. Thus the French term "giboyeuse" in *Dans la pluie giboyeuse*, literally, "In the Game-Filled Rain," was finally rendered by "In the Quarried Rain," so that the "quarry" of this future prey brought with it the other notion of quarry, not present in the actual title, but running throughout Char's work: "l'équarisseur" or the figure of the quarterer, is of the same stature as the tree-pruner or the sailmaker, serving as their dark counterpart. The rule of literality was adhered to, and remained the most reliable guiding criterion; finally it was made to converge with an intuition about the sense of these poems, after much thought and many discussions with the poet.

Some of the changes away from a literal transcription were made at his suggestion: occasional inversions, minor shifts in terminology, almost imperceptible ellipses, and slightly differing topography or typography. For example, the punctuation of the title "Qu'il vive!" has become "Long live. . .", a change that opens the title and the poem itself in a different way. Similarly, in the poem by far the most demanding of those undertaken by this translator, "Le Visage nuptial," whose rendering went through more than twelve versions over a long period, quite a few of the more erotic images have come through in English with a different slant, because of the striking difference in the specific vocabulary. The individual problems have at last been submerged within the whole, and by exception—for this poem is exceptional in many ways—the one example we are prompted to give is a positive one. A central term, "plaisir," was altered to read "joy," at René Char's suggestion, for "pleasure" was too light-hearted and too trivial for the grave and joyous eroticism of the line and of the poem.

Throughout this work of deepening correspondence, between the poem and its interpreter, we found ourselves called upon to bring to bear on each decision all we had at hand from a prolonged reading not only of this poet but of others: that the translations, like the reading, will never *suffice* is a fact not to be anguished over, but rather to be welcomed, for it is the only assurance we have that the poem will remain open also in English.

Now from the texts that emerged, imperfect but tried and tempered in the exhausting and marvelous struggle between the languages, not only English and French, but also the language of greatly differing personalities, this struggle as if between two "mortal partners" (to quote the title of a prose poem), one single pronoun may offer a résumé of the recurring difficulty, which it illustrates, illuminates, and to which in some sense it gives a wider implicit meaning. In the brief circular poem of "Allégeance," the French pronoun "il" for "mon amour" found no equivalent capable of retaining the original ambiguity. For the subject of the poem is, in fact, "my love," neither a "she" nor a coldly neutral "it." In the end, there was no choice other than the latter, precisely because of the essential focus of the poem on love itself, rather than on the person loved. It has to be understood, or rather to be hoped, that the very oddness of this choice will draw the reader's attention to the ambiguity, clearly visible in the facing French text. Briefly, if we had to define our object in these translations of René Char, we could do no better than this: to call attention to the opposite page. It is also, it goes without saying, a grave risk, since the partners could never have matched exactly. And yet, ideally, the poem and its translation would not signal a betrayal of the first by the second, but would share at last the same countenance, having shared the same mortal struggle—whether this countenance is troubled in its fragmentation, as in *Le Poème pulvérisé*, or redeemed, as in "Le Visage nuptial." If the translations themselves are also a *Recherche de la base et du sommet* and a *Retour amont*, it is toward this only possible summit that they would hope to lead. For these texts are arranged, in consultation with the poet, along the path of his, and our, return upland.[7]

And, no matter what our doubts, the poet's faith in his poem must also be ours. If a meaning is lost from the original word, says René Char, the balance will be restored later; the poem will always right itself. Its own light will compensate for our omissions, rectifying a temporary swerve to one side

---

[7] The most recent Italian translations are entitled: *Ritorno sopramonte*, after the collection *Retour amont* (Lo Specchio, Mondadori, 1974, translated by Vittorio Sereni, preface by Jean Starobinski). The notes for this volume are particularly recommended.

or another of a meaning. "The poem is, in the act of making itself. It is never made. . . ."[8] The poet's profound explanation of his always active voice reaches past its seeming specificity to the entire universe he envisions, complete in each poem, and which, in their unique privilege, the translator, and the reader also, must now make their own.

MARY ANN CAWS, *January, 1975*

* * *

The poems of René Char have no need of being praised to anyone who reads them. This book exists to help more people read them. If it is good enough it will, we hope, bring many more English-speaking readers into direct contact with the poetry of René Char. It gives a quite large selection of the original poems with translations on facing pages; and the object of each translation is, as Mary Ann Caws puts it, "to draw attention to the opposite page."

What more is there to say? René Char himself suggested one thing. When I submitted to him an attempt at a preface, he quoted back at me, from a letter of mine, the words "traduire c'est lire en profondeur"—translating is reading in depth—and went on to say that "the true knowledge, the one that lasts for the reader of a book of poems, would be that you, a poet, should tell us about what you do, step by step, when you carry into your language a foreign poet. . . ." So here are a few workshop notes.

Sometimes a difference of usage between the two languages can give trouble. The title of the second *Lascaux* poem is *Les cerfs noirs*. For this I put "The black stag," because in British hunting circles the plural of "stag" is "stag." Still, there are several black stag in the frieze of the Lascaux cave, and in the poem. How to convey this? Not in the title, but by be-

[8] Correspondence.

ginning the second line with: "Stag, you and you and you have crossed millennia. . ."

That example does not go deep: I select it because usage is important. A poem means all of what it says, and a translator's job is to convey this all, without getting heavy, musclebound, unmusical. The poetry of Char presents this problem at its extreme: most poems by Char say such a formidable amount in a few words that they often read unlike anything else, prose or verse. Translations of them will rightly be no less extreme, and because of this a translator of Char has to keep especially alert never to hinder the reader by departing from usage without good reason. When there is a chance of combining fidelity to the content's riches with flow and lightness, one must take it. It helps to render the agility of these poems, which matches their weight.

Now for an example that does go deep—in "La bibliothèque est en feu," that nuclear sentence, "L'éclair me dure." After various tries, I decided on "Lightning lasts me." The author objected that "lasts" renders only one of the meanings here combined, one of these being that "lightning goes on in me, it drives deep into me, it finds in me its echo land," the other that "lightning makes me last, it fertilizes me, it feeds my distances." And again: "lighting continues me, I continue the lightning." (Later, characteristically, he wrote: "I must have added one or two that did not come into my mind at the time.") To keep the transitive force he suggested "perdures" or "abides." I wrote back that I think "Lightning lasts me" does comprise pretty well all the meanings, and

> it hits hard, first because "lasts" is a monosyllable, but also because "lasts" resembles and is not "blasts"—the reader will quite likely expect the conventional "blasts," find himself confronted by "lasts" and be forced to reflect, to pursue the meanings, the resonances, to listen to that thunder.

I said that "abides" would, unfortunately, suggest "I can't abide him." As for "perdures," it's a marvelous Shakespearean word that has gone out of use and would, I'm afraid, here produce a pastiche effect: it would express all the meanings of the original as much as (not more than) "lasts": in short, a temptation we ought to resist.[1]

So "lasts" was accepted. Yet I still wonder: "Lightning perdures me" (René Char's suggestion), besides being faithful, is strong and grand. Is the danger of alienating readers who may take it as an archaism a good reason for sacrificing it? Hard to decide.

In "Yvonne," the word "manoeuvre" gave me trouble. First I put "drill." The author pointed out that there is "all the intelligence of the hand" in the word "manoeuvre"—"the notion of 'handling,' 'managing,' 'dealing with.' " I tried "handiwork" and "craft"—hesitantly, for they did not seem to come to life, and in fact René Char wrote that they were "too limitative" and added:

> This word must be taken figuratively, as a revalorisation in every sense, moral as well as emotional, of that power of accomplishing and aiding which some people in this world have. "Yvonne" was one of those.

With this help I found "common task," the phrase from John Keble's hymn which so many of us have sung in church and chapel. This was warmly accepted.

The last poem in the sequence *Against a Dry House* contains the word "dieux-dits," an invented word. My first attempt was: "Their godships delegate their leisure to us for a short while. . . ." Explanation came: that "dieux-dits" is analogous to "lieux-dits," which means "a small locality, often a cluster of houses, a hamlet," and that "the general image is that of the cluster, the archipelago," as in the title of Char's book *La Parole en archipel*. This showed what to search for. Result: "godsteads."

---

[1] His letters and mine were in French; the quotations from them are translated.

Rarely of course, but sometimes, the dialogue between the original poet and the translator can turn up a word or a phrase that comes even nearer than the original did to what was really, yet in part unconsciously, intended. I first translated "Prince des contresens"—the opening words of *Le serpent*—as "Prince of contradictions." That was not what René Char meant, and in a letter he asked if there was not a word in English closer to "contre-sens." I suggested "Prince of anti-order," and this he generously described as excellent, "d'un point de plus dans l'arrière-pays, dans l'inconscient du vouloir dire" (one point closer into the back country, into the unconscious of meaning).

These examples show that translating fine poetry is a creative and joyful business, like the interpretation of music, which is discovery of what the composer meant.

JONATHAN GRIFFIN, *January, 1975*

XXX

POEMS OF

RENÉ CHAR

LE MARTEAU SANS MAITRE suivi de MOULIN PREMIER

1927-1934

THE HAMMER WITH NO MASTER followed by
FIRST MILL

1927-1934

Vers quelle mer enragée, ignorée même des poètes, pouvait bien s'en aller, aux environs de 1930, ce fleuve mal aperçu qui coulait dans des terres où les accords de la fertilité déjà se mouraient, où l'allégorie de l'horreur commençait à se concrétiser, ce fleuve radiant et énigmatique baptisé Marteau sans Maître? *Vers l'hallucinante expérience de l'homme noué au Mal, de l'homme massacré et pourtant victorieux.*

La clef du Marteau sans Maître *tourne dans la réalité pressentie des années 1937-1944. Le premier rayon qu'elle délivre hésite entre l'imprécation du supplice et le magnifique amour.*

(Feuillet pour la 2ᵉ édition, 1945)

2

Toward what enraged sea, unknown even to poets, could this river, scarcely even perceived, have been flowing, around 1930, coursing through lands where the covenants of fertility were already expiring, where the allegory of horror was beginning to take on concrete existence—this radiant and enigmatic river baptized The Hammer with No Master? *Toward the hallucinating experience of man riveted to evil, of man massacred and still victorious.*

The key of The Hammer with No Master *turns in the reality of the years 1937-1944, foreshadowed. The first ray it gives forth hesitates between the imprecation of agony and a magnificent love.*

(Preface for second edition, 1945)

M.A.C.

Robustes météores

Dans le bois on écoute bouillir le ver
La chrysalide tournant au clair visage
Sa délivrance naturelle

Les hommes ont faim
De viandes secrètes d'outils cruels
Levez-vous bêtes à égorger
A gagner le soleil.

A l'horizon remarquable

Les grands chemins
Dorment à l'ombre de ses mains

Elle marche au supplice
Demain
Comme une traînée de poudre.

Bel édifice et les pressentiments

J'écoute marcher dans mes jambes
La mer morte vagues par-dessus tête

Enfant la jetée-promenade sauvage
Homme l'illusion imitée

Des yeux purs dans les bois
Cherchent en pleurant la tête habitable.

4

Robust Meteors

In the wood we listen to the worm boiling
The chrysalis turning toward a clear face
Its natural deliverance

Men are hungry
For secret meats for cruel implements
Rise up beasts to slaughter
To reach the sun.

M.A.C.

On the Remarkable Horizon

The high roads
Sleep in the shade of her hands

She walks to her torment
Tomorrow
Like wildfire

M.A.C.

Fine Building and Forebodings

I hear moving in my steps a sea long-dead
Waves overhead

As a child, the wild jetty-walk
As a man the illusion imitated

Pure eyes in the woods
Seek weeping the head to dwell in.

5

Sosie

Animal
A l'aide de pierres
Efface mes longues pelisses

Homme
Je n'ose pas me servir
Des pierres qui te ressemblent

Animal
Gratte avec tes ongles
Ma chair est d'une rude écorce

Homme
J'ai peur du feu
Partout où tu te trouves

Animal
Tu parles
Comme un homme

Détrompe-toi
Je ne vais pas au bout de ton dénuement.

Double

Animal
With the help of stones
Raze my long fur

Man
I dare not use
Stones which resemble you

Animal
Scratch with your claws
My flesh is rough bark

Man
I am afraid of fire
Wherever you may be

Animal
You speak
Like a man

Make no mistake
I'll not go to the limit of your destitution.

M.A.C.

Artine

Au silence de celle qui laisse rêveur.

*Dans le lit qu'on m'avait préparé il y avait: un animal san-
guinolent et meurtri, de la taille d'une brioche, un tuyau
de plomb, une rafale de vent, un coquillage glacé, une car-
touche tirée, deux doigts d'un gant, une tache d'huile; il n'y
avait pas de porte de prison, il y avait le goût de l'amer-
tume, un diamant de vitrier, un cheveu, un jour, une chaise
cassée, un ver à soie, l'objet volé, une chaîne de pardessus,
une mouche verte apprivoisée, une branche de corail, un
clou de cordonnier, une roue d'omnibus.*

Offrir au passage un verre d'eau à un cavalier lancé à
bride abattue sur un hippodrome envahi par la foule sup-
pose, de part et d'autre, un manque absolu d'adresse; Ar-
tine apportait aux esprits qu'elle visitait cette sécheresse
monumentale.

L'impatient se rendait parfaitement compte de l'ordre
des rêves qui hanteraient dorénavant son cerveau, surtout
dans le domaine de l'amour où l'activité dévorante se
manifestait couramment en dehors du temps sexuel;
l'assimilation se développant, la nuit noire, dans les serres
bien closes.

Artine traverse sans difficulté le nom d'une ville. C'est le
silence qui détache le sommeil.

Les objets désignés et rassemblés sous le nom de nature-
précise font partie du décor dans lequel se déroulent les
actes d'érotisme des *suites fatales,* épopée quotidienne et
nocturne. Les mondes imaginaires chauds qui circulent
sans arrêt dans la campagne à l'époque des moissons ren-
dent l'œil agressif et la solitude intolérable à celui qui dis-
pose du pouvoir de destruction. Pour les extraordinaires
bouleversements il est tout de même préférable de s'en
remettre entièrement à eux.

Artine (1930)

To the silence of one who leaves us dreaming.

In the bed prepared for me were: an animal bruised and slightly bleeding, no larger than a bun, a lead pipe, a gust of wind, an icy seashell, a spent cartridge, two fingers of a glove, a spot of oil; there was no prison door, rather the taste of bitterness, a glazier's diamond, one hair, one day, a broken chair, a silkworm, the stolen object, an over-coat chain, a tame green fly, a branch of coral, a cob-bler's nail, a bus wheel.

To offer a glass of water to a horseman as he passes hurtling headlong on a racetrack invaded by the mob takes an absolute awkwardness on both sides; Artine brought to the minds she visited this monumental drought.

Impatient, he was perfectly aware of the order of dreams which would henceforth haunt his brain, espe-cially in the realm of love whose devouring activities usu-ally appeared in other than sexual moments; assimilation developing, through the dead of darkness, in hothouses closed tight.

Artine traverses effortlessly the name of a town. Silence unleashes sleep.

The objects described by and gathered under the name of *nature-précise*[1] form part of the setting for erotic acts bound to *fatal consequences*, an epic daily and nocturnal. Hot imaginary worlds circulating ceaselessly in the coun-tryside at harvest-time render the eye aggressive and soli-tude intolerable to the wielder of destructive power. For extraordinary upheavals, however, it is preferable to rely altogether upon them.

---

[1] Here the term plays on "nature morte" or still-life.

L'état de léthargie qui précédait Artine apportait les éléments indispensables à la projection d'impressions saisissantes sur l'écran de ruines flottantes: édredon en flammes précipité dans l'insondable gouffre de ténèbres en perpétuel mouvement.

Artine gardait en dépit des animaux et des cyclones une intarissable fraîcheur. A la promenade, c'était la transparence absolue.

A beau surgir au milieu de la plus active dépression l'appareil de la beauté d'Artine, les esprits curieux demeurent des esprits furieux, les esprits indifférents des esprits extrêmement curieux.

Les apparitions d'Artine dépassaient le cadre de ces contrées du sommeil, où le *pour* et le *pour* sont animés d'une égale et meurtrière violence. Elles évoluaient dans les plis d'une soie brûlante peuplée d'arbres aux feuilles de cendre.

La voiture à chevaux lavée et remise à neuf l'emportait presque toujours sur l'appartement tapissé de salpêtre lorsqu'il s'agissait d'accueillir durant une soirée interminable la multitude des ennemis mortels d'Artine. Le visage de bois mort était particulièrement odieux. La course haletante de deux amants au hasard des grands chemins devenait tout à coup une distraction suffisante pour permettre au drame de se dérouler, derechef, à ciel ouvert.

Quelquefois une manœuvre maladroite faisait tomber sur la gorge d'Artine une tête qui n'était pas la mienne. L'énorme bloc de soufre se consumait alors lentement, sans fumée, présence en soi et immobilité vibrante.

Le livre ouvert sur les genoux d'Artine était seulement lisible les jours sombres. A intervalles irréguliers les héros venaient apprendre les malheurs qui allaient à nouveau fondre sur eux, les voies multiples et terrifiantes dans lesquelles leur irréprochable destinée allait à nouveau s'engager. Uniquement soucieux de la Fatalité, ils étaient pour la plupart d'un physique agréable. Ils se déplaçaient avec

The lethargic state preceding Artine added what was indispensable to the projection of striking impressions onto the screen of floating ruins: eiderdown in flames cast into the unfathomable abyss of perpetually moving shadows.

In spite of animals and cyclones, Artine retained an inexhaustible freshness. On outings, this was the most absolute transparency.

From the most active depression, the array of Artine's beauty may arise, but the curious minds remain nevertheless furious, the indifferent minds extremely curious.

Artine's appearances went past the border of those countries of sleep where the *for* and the *for* are endowed with an equal and murderous violence. They occurred in the folds of a burning silk peopled with ashen-leaved trees.

Washed and renovated, the horse-drawn chariot nearly always won out over the saltpeter-papered apartment playing host for an interminable evening to the multitude of Artine's mortal enemies. The dead-wood face was particularly odious. The breathless race of two lovers at random along the highways suddenly became a diversion sufficient for a dramatic unfolding thereupon, out in the open air.

Sometimes, a careless movement caused a head other than mine to sink on Artine's breast. The enormous sulphur block consumed its substance slowly and smokelessly, presence in itself vibrating motionless.

The book open on Artine's knees could be read only on somber days. At irregular intervals heroes would come to learn the calamities once more to befall them, and in what numerous and fearful directions their irreproachable fate would start out afresh. Concerned only with Fatality, they presented for the most part an agreeable appear-lenteur, se montraient peu loquaces. Ils exprimaient leurs désirs à l'aide de larges mouvements de tête imprévisibles. Ils paraissaient en outre s'ignorer totalement entre eux.

Le poète a tué son modèle.

ance. They moved about slowly and were not loquacious. They expressed their desires in broad unforeseeable motions of their heads. Moreover, they seemed to be utterly unconscious of each other.

The poet has slain his model.

M.A.C.

Poètes

La tristesse des illettrés dans les ténèbres des bouteilles
L'inquiétude imperceptible des charrons
Les pièces de monnaie dans la vase profonde

Dans les nacelles de l'enclume
Vit le poète solitaire
Grande brouette des marécages.

Poets

Sadness of illiterates in the shadows of bottles
Cartwrights' imperceptible disquiet
Coins in deep slime

In the skiffs of the anvil
The poet lives solitary
Great wheelbarrow of marshlands

M.A.C.

15

La luxure

L'aigle voit de plus en plus s'effacer les pistes de la
    mémoire gelée
L'étendue de solitude rend à peine visible la proie filante
A travers chacune des régions
Où l'on tue où l'on est tué sans contrainte
Proie insensible
Projetée indistinctement
En deçà du désir et au delà de la mort

Le rêveur embaumé dans sa camisole de force
Entouré d'outils temporaires
Figures aussitôt évanouies que composées
Leur révolution célèbre l'apothéose de la vie déclinante
La disparition progressive des parties léchées
La chute des torrents dans l'opacité des tombeaux
Les sueurs et les malaises annonciateurs du feu central
L'univers enfin de toute sa poitrine athlétique
Nécropole fluviale
Après le déluge des sourciers

Ce fanatique des nuages
A le pouvoir surnaturel
De déplacer sur des distances considérables
Les paysages habituels
De rompre l'harmonie agglomérée
De rendre méconnaissables les lieux funèbres
Au lendemain des meurtres productifs
Sans que la conscience originelle
Se couvre du purificateur glissement de terrain.

Lust

The eagle sees the tracks of frozen memory growing ever
    fainter
The stretch of solitude renders scarcely visible the fleeting
    prey
Across each of the regions
Where you slay or are slain with no constraint
Insensitive prey
Hazily projected
On this side of desire and on that side of death

The dreamer embalmed in his straitjacket
Surrounded with temporary implements
Figures faded as soon as composed
Their revolution extols the apotheosis of life ebbing
The progressive vanishing of licked parts
The tumble of torrents into the opacity of tombs
Sweats and unease heralds of the central fire
Finally the universe with its athlete chest
Fluvial necropolis
After the deluge of water-diviners

This fanatic of clouds
Displaces supernaturally over considerable distances
Customary landscapes
Disrupts harmony agglomerate
Renders the funereal haunts unrecognizable
On the morrow of productive murders
Without a purifying landslide
Overcasting first awareness

M.A.C.

17

Chaine

Le grand bûcher des alliances
Sous le spiral ciel d'échec
C'est l'hiver en barque pourrie
Des compagnons solides aux compagnes liquides
Des lits de mort sous les écorces
Dans les profondeurs vacantes de la terre
Les arcs forgent un nouveau nombre d'ailes
Les labours rayonnants adorent les guérisseurs détrempés
Sur la paille des fatalistes
L'écume d'astre coule tout allumée
Il n'y a pas d'absence irremplaçable.

Vivante demain

Par la grande échappée du mur
Je t'ai reçue votive des mains de l'hiver

Je te regardais traversant les anneaux de sable des
    cuirasses
Comme la génération des mélancoliques le préau des jeux

Sur l'herbe de plomb
Sur l'herbe de mâchefer
Sur l'herbe jamais essoufflée
Hors de laquelle la ressemblance des brûlures avec
    leur fatalité n'est jamais parfaite
Faisons l'amour.

18

Chain

The great funeral-pyre of joinings
Under the spiral failure sky
Is winter in a rotted boat
From solid comrades to liquid companions
Death beds beneath tree bark
In earth's vacant depths
Arches forge wings in fresh quantity
Radiant tillage adores the sodden healers
On the straw of fatalists
The foam of stars flows fully lit
There is no absence irreplaceable.

M.A.C.

Alive Tomorrow

Through the wall's wide gap
I received you votive from winter's hands

I saw you traversing the sand rings of breastplates
As did the generation of melancholies the courtyard of
    games

On the grass of lead
On the grass of slag
On the grass never breathless
Past which the likeness of burns to their fate is never
    exact.
Let us make love.

M.A.C.

19

L'éclaircie

La vase sur la peau des reins, le gravier sur le nerf op-
tique, tolérance et contenance. Absolue aridité, tu as ab-
sorbé toute la mémoire individuelle en la traversant. Tu
t'es établie dans le voisinage des fontaines, autour de la
conque, ce guêpier. Tu rumines. Tu t'orientes. Souveraine
et mère d'un grand muet, l'homme te voit dans son rasoir,
la compensation de sa disgrâce, d'une dynastie essentielle.

L'invincible dormeur enseignait que là où le mica était
perméable aux larmes la présence de la mer ne s'expliquait
pas. De nos jours, les mêmes oisifs distinguent dans les
fraîches cervelles innocentes les troubles insurmontables
de l'âge futur. Symptômes de l'angoisse à l'extérieur des
sépultures de l'ingénuité en extase; — ô profanation de
l'esprit thermidor de famille, aurons-nous le temps de vous
imposer notre grandeur?—L'inacte chrysalide a recouvré
ses propriétés agissantes de vertige. La perforation des
cellules du rayon, la traversée de la cheminée anathé-
matisée, la reconnaissance des créances oubliées se pour-
suivent à travers les éclairs, le grésillement et la révélation
de l'espèce fulgurante de grain solaire. Le sort de l'imagi-
nation adhérant sans réserves au développement d'un
monde en tout renouvelé de l'attractif pourra être déter-
miné en cours de fouilles dans les archipels de l'estomac,
à la suite de la brutale montée, à l'intelligence non sou-
mise, du trésor sismique des famines.

Clearing

Mire on the skin of loins, gravel on the optic nerve, tolerance and countenance. Absolute aridity, you've absorbed all individual memory, traversing it. You've settled in the neighborhood of fountains, around the conch shell, that hornets' nest. You ruminate. You take your bearings. Sovereign and mother of a great mute, man sees you in his razor, compensating for his disgrace, of an essential dynasty.

It was the teaching of the invincible sleeper that where the mica was permeable to tears the sea's presence was unexplained. Nowadays, the same idlers discern in fresh and innocent brains the future's insuperable confusion. Marks of anguish traced upon tombs of ecstatic ingenuity;—oh profanation of the thermidor family spirit, shall we have time to impose our greatness upon you?—The unbroken chrysalis has recovered its active vertiginous properties. The perforation of honeycomb cells, the crossing of the anathematized chimney, the acknowledgement of forgotten claims chase one another through the flashes, crackling and revelation of the fulgurant species of sun squall. The fate of imagination adhering unreservedly to the development of a world completely renewed in its attraction may be determined during excavations in intestinal archipelagoes, following the brutal ascent, uncontrolled by intelligence, of the seismic treasure of famines.

M.A.C.

Migration

Le poids du raisin modifie la position des feuilles. La montagne avait un peu glissé. Sans dégager d'époque. Toutefois, à travers les ossuaires argileux, la foulée des bêtes excrémentielles en marche vers le convulsif ambre jaune. En relation avec l'inerte.

La sécurité est un parfum. L'homme morne et emblématique vit toujours en prison, mais sa prison se trouve à présent en liberté. Le mouvement et le sentiment ont réintégré la fronde mathématicienne. La fabuleuse simulatrice, celle qui s'ensevelit en marchant, qui remporta dans la nuit tragique de la préhistoire les quatre doigts tabous de la main-fantôme, a rejoint ses quartiers d'étude, à la zone des clairvoyances. Dans le salon manqué, sur les grands carreaux hostiles, le dormeur et l'aimée, trop impopulaires pour ne pas être réels, accouplent interminablement leurs bouches ruisselantes de salive.

22

Migration

To Yvonne Zervos

The weight of the grape alters the leaves' position. The mountain had slipped a little. Without unearthing an epoch. Nevertheless, across the clay ossuaries, the tread of excremental beasts in their progress toward the convulsive yellow amber. In relation with the inert.

Security is a perfume. Drab and emblematic man still lives imprisoned, but his prison has been given its freedom. Movement and feeling have reintegrated the mathematical sling-shot. The fabulous simulator, who interred herself while walking, carrying back into the tragic night of prehistory the four taboo fingers on the phantom hand, has returned to her study, within the zone of clairvoyance. In the unsuccessful living room, on the great hostile tiles, the sleeper and the beloved, so greatly disliked that they must be real, endlessly couple their mouths streaming with saliva.

M.A.C.

Moulin premier (extraits)

*Il faut ici, contradiction qui paraît sans issue,
il faut ici, de toute nécessité, l'immobilité de la
mort et la fraîcheur d'entrailles de la vie.*
—J.-H. FABRE

IV

Aptitude: porteur d'alluvions en flamme.

Audace d'être un instant soi-même la forme accomplie
du poème. Bien-être d'avoir entrevu scintiller la matière-
émotion instantanément reine.

XV

Je ne plaisante pas avec les porcs.

XVIII

Le canal s'avance au-devant du fleuve. Tous deux égaux
en profondeur, tous deux égaux devant l'aurore.

A toi, tout entier à toi, à genoux, soumis sur le passage
de tes processions hors-nature, ô mon amour abîmé, mor-
dant dans un silo de chaude vase frénétique.

(Nous aimions les eaux opaques, prétendues polluées,
qui n'étaient le miroir d'aucun ciel levant, les parfums ras
intégralement respirés et ce fond de teint de la mort en sen-
tinelle adossée, débonnairement présente.)

XXV

Cédez au sommeil, haute génération matinale du linge.
Le mouvement des clartés aboutit au plaisir.

XXXIII

L'oscillation d'un auteur derrière son oeuvre, c'est de
la pure toilette matérialiste.

24

First Mill (extracts)

> *We must have here, a contradiction apparently inescapable, we absolutely must have death's immobility and the freshness of life's entrails.*
> —J.-H. FABRE

IV

Aptitude: bearer of alluvia ablaze.

Daring to be for an instant oneself the accomplished form of the poem. Comfort of having glimpsed matter-emotion sparkling instantly queen.

XV

I do not banter with pigs.

XVIII

The canal goes forward to meet the river. Both equal in depth, both equal in the face of dawn.

Yours, entirely yours, on my knees, humble at the passing of your unnatural processions, oh my damaged love, biting in a silo of hot frenetic slime.

(We loved the opaque waters, said to be polluted, which were the mirror of no rising sky, bare perfumes wholly breathed and this foundation cream of death, a sentinel leaning back, mildly present.)

XXV

Give in to sleep, high matinal generation of linen. The motion of brightness ends in pleasure.

XXXIII

The oscillation of an author behind his work, nothing other than materialistic grooming.

XXXVII

Il advient au poète d'échouer au cours de ses recherches sur un rivage où il n'était attendu que beaucoup plus tard, après son anéantissement. Insensible à l'hostilité de son entourage arriéré le poète s'organise, abat sa vigueur, morcèle le terme, agrafe les sommets des ailes.

XLVIII

Les longues promenades silencieuses, à deux, la nuit, à travers la campagne déserte, en compagnie de la panthère somnambule, terreur des maçons.

LXVIII

Le feu se communique au son du pain des cuisses.
O touffe élargie! ô beauté
Instable longtemps contrariée de l'évidence,
Main-d'œuvre errante de moi-même!

26

XXXVII

The poet happens to land during the course of his seekings on a shore where he was not expected until much later, after his extinction. Insensitive to the hostility of his backward companions, the poet makes preparations, fells his vigor, divides the term, fastens the summits of his wings.

XLVIII

The long silent walks together at night, across the deserted countryside, in the company of the sleepwalking panther, the masons' terror.

LXVIII

At the sound of the bread of thighs, fire spreads.
Oh widened tuft! oh unstable
Beauty contradicted at length by evidence,
Wandering handcraft of myself!

M.A.C.

27

Commune présence

I

Eclaireur comme tu surviens tard
L'arbre a châtié une à une ses feuilles
La terre à bec-de-lièvre a bu le dévoué sourire
Je t'écoutais au menu jour gravir la croisée
Où s'émiette au-dessus de l'indifférence des chiens
La toute pure image expérimentale du crime en voie de
   fossilisation
Qui prête au bienveillant les rumeurs de l'hostile
A l'irréfléchi le destin du mutiné?
L'inhumain ne s'est pas servilement converti
Au comptoir des mots enchantés
Indiscernable il rôde sur le tracé des flaques
Et gouverne selon son sang
Gardien de sa raison de son amour de son butin de son
   oubli de sa révolte de ses certitudes

Charpente constellée
Sont-ils épris de leur propre mort
Au point de ne pouvoir de leur vivant l'attribuant
Se démettre déborder d'elle. . .

Shared Presence

I

Light-bearer how late you come
The tree chastised its leaves one by one
The hare-lipped earth drank the devoted smile
I listened to you climbing the casement in the morning
   twilight
Where above the dogs' indifference crumbles
The purest experimental image of crime being fossilized
Who attributes to the obliging the rumble of the adverse
To the thoughtless the fate of the mutinous?
The inhuman one has not converted slavishly
At the counter of enchanted words
Indiscernible he prowls on the tracing of pools
And governs according to his blood
Keeper of his reason his love his plunder his forgetting
   his rebellion his certainties.

Construction bestarred
Are they so enamored of their own death
That they cannot living assume it
To resign or overflow beyond . . .

II

Tu es pressé d'écrire
Comme si tu étais en retard sur la vie
S'il en est ainsi fais cortège à tes sources
Hâte-toi
Hâte-toi de transmettre
Ta part de merveilleux de rébellion de bienfaisance
Effectivement tu es en retard sur la vie
La vie inexprimable
La seule en fin de compte à laquelle tu acceptes de t'unir
Celle qui t'est refusée chaque jour par les êtres et par les
    choses
Dont tu obtiens péniblement deci delà quelques fragments
    décharnés
Au bout de combats sans merci
Hors d'elle tout n'est qu'agonie soumise fin grossière
Si tu rencontres la mort durant ton labeur
Reçois-la comme la nuque en sueur trouve bon le
    mouchoir aride
En t'inclinant
Si tu veux rire
Offre ta soumission
Jamais tes armes
Tu as été créé pour des moments peu communs
Modifie-toi disparais sans regret
Au gré de la rigueur suave
Quartier suivant quartier la liquidation du monde se
    poursuit
Sans interruption
Sans égarement

Essaime la poussière
Nul ne décèlera votre union.

II

You are in a rush to write
As if you were of a slower pace than life
If this be so accompany your sources
Hasten
Hasten to transmit
Your portion of wonder rebellion good-will
In truth you are behind in life
Life inexpressible
The only one you accept at last to join with
Alone refused you every day by beings and by things
Whence you take laboriously here and there a few fleshless
    fragments
After implacable struggles
Beyond it, agony humbled, rude end
If you meet death as you toil
Receive it as the perspiring neck welcomes the arid
    kerchief
Yielding
If you choose to laugh
Offer your submission
Never your weapons
You were created for rare moments
Change disappear unregretful
At the will of sweet severity
Quarter upon quarter the world continues its liquidation
Without interruption
Without distraction

Let dust swarm—
None will divulge your union.

M.A.C.

DEHORS LA NUIT EST GOUVERNEE
précédé de
PLACARD POUR UN CHEMIN DES ECOLIERS

1936-1938

OUTSIDE THE NIGHT IS RULED
preceded by
SIGN FOR A SCHOOLCHILD'S WAY

1936-1938

Compagnie de l'écolière

Je sais bien que les chemins marchent
Plus vite que les écoliers
Attelés à leur cartable
Roulant dans la glu des fumées
Où l'automne perd le souffle
Jamais douce à vos sujets
Est-ce vous que j'ai vue sourire
Ma fille ma fille je tremble

N'aviez-vous donc pas méfiance
De ce vagabond étranger
Quand il enleva sa casquette
Pour vous demander son chemin
Vous n'avez pas paru surprise
Vous vous êtes abordés
Comme coquelicot et blé
Ma fille ma fille je tremble

La fleur qu'il tient entre les dents
Il pourrait la laisser tomber
S'il consent à donner son nom
A rendre l'épave à ses vagues
Ensuite quelque aveu maudit
Qui hanterait votre sommeil
Parmi les ajoncs de son sang
Ma fille ma fille je tremble

Quand ce jeune homme s'éloigna
Le soir mura votre visage
Quand ce jeune homme s'éloigna
Dos voûté front bas et mains vides
Sous les osiers vous étiez grave
Vous ne l'aviez jamais été
Vous rendra-t-il votre beauté
Ma fille ma fille je tremble

A Schoolgirl, Her Company

Yes I know the roads walk
Faster than children out of school
Who harnessed to their satchels wallow
In the mire of the mists of smoke
Where the autumn loses its breath
Never gentle to your subjects
Is it you I just saw smile
Daughter daughter I am afraid

Had you not learned to have no faith
In that stranger vagabond
When he raised his cap and bowed
Before asking you the way
That seemed no surprise to you
You came together then you two
Like the poppy and the wheat
Daughter daughter I am afraid

The flower he holds between his teeth
He may well let fall that bloom
If he consents to tell his name
To give the wreck back to its waves
Then lets some damned avowal slip
Out and about to haunt your sleep
Among the thorns of his blood's broom
Daughter daughter I am afraid

As that young man moved away
Evening walled your features in
As that young man moved away
(Low forehead round back empty hands)
Under the osiers you were grave
That is a thing you've never been
Will he give you your beauty again
Daughter daughter I am afraid

La fleur qu'il gardait à la bouche
Savez-vous ce qu'elle cachait
Père un mal pur bordé de mouches
Je l'ai voilé de ma pitié
Mais ses yeux tenaient la promesse
Que je me suis faite à moi-même
Je suis folle je suis nouvelle
C'est vous mon père qui changez.

The flower he still saved in his mouth
Do you know what lay hid in it
Father a pure pain ringed with flies
I have veiled it in my pity
But he was keeping with his eyes
The promise I've made to myself
I am mad I am new
It's you father altering now.

J.G.

Courbet: les casseurs de cailloux

Sable paille ont la vie douce le vin ne s'y brise pas
Du colombier ils récoltent les plumes
De la goulotte ils ont la langue avide
Ils retardent l'orteil des filles
Dont ils percent les chrysalides
Le sang bien souffert tombe dans l'anecdote de leur
    légèreté

Nous dévorons la peste du feu gris dans la rocaille
Quand on intrigue à la commune
C'est encore sur les chemins ruinés qu'on est le mieux
Là les tomates des vergers l'air nous les porte au
    crépuscule
Avec l'oubli de la méchanceté prochaine de nos femmes
Et l'aigreur de la soif tassée aux genoux

Fils cette nuit nos travaux de poussière
Seront visibles dans le ciel
Déjà l'huile du plomb ressuscite.

Courbet: The Stone-breakers[2]

Sand, straw, have an easy life, wine doesn't shatter in
   them
They gather feathers from the dovecote
Their tongue is eager for the gullet
They slow the girl's toes going
Whose chrysalids they pierce
Blood fitly suffered falls in talkative lightness

In the rock we devour the grey fire's plague
When gossip spreads in the commune
We fare better even on ruined paths
There, a breeze brings us orchard tomatoes at twilight
A disregard for our wives' next nastiness
And thirst's sharp taste amassed in our knees

Son, tonight, our works of dust
Will be visible in the sky
Already oil returns to life from lead.

                                     M.A.C.

[2] Of Courbet's two canvases by this name, the poem refers to the
one in the Dresden museum, destroyed in the war; it represented
an older man and a younger, working on a road.

Une italienne de Corot

Sur le ruisseau à la crue grise
Une portière garance s'est soulevée
Ma chair reste au bord du sillon

A moissonner des tiges on se plie on raisonne l'ignoré
La percale me boit et le drap me prolonge
Contre les lèvres du vallon je languis

Lorsqu'ils s'entourent de distances qui découragent
Je tends la vigueur de mes bras à l'écume des moribonds
J'applique ma loi blanche à leur front
Je suis à qui m'assaille je cède au poids furieux
L'air de mes longues veines est inépuisable

Je m'écarte de l'odeur des bergers
De mon toit je distingue la rue ses pavés qui ricanent

Une haie d'érables se rabat chez un peintre qui l'ébranche
   sur la paix de sa toile
C'est un familier des fermes pauvres
Affable et chagrin comme un scarabée.

An Italian Girl by Corot

On the stream grey-swelling
A madder-red curtain rose
My flesh remains on the furrow's edge

To harvest stalks you bend, you argue with the over-
    looked
Percale drinks me and the sheet prolongs me
Against the valley's lips I languish

When they are bordered with discouraging distance
I stretch my arms' force to the froth of the moribund
Applying my white law to their forehead
I belong to my assailant, I succumb to furious
    pressure
The air of my long veins inexhaustible

I withdraw from the smell of shepherds
From my roof I sight the street, its stones sneering

A line of maples takes shelter with a painter pruning it
    into the peace of his canvas
He's a frequenter of indigent farms
Affable and downcast like a scarab.

                                        M.A.C.

Remise

Laissez filer les guides, maintenant c'est la plaine
Il gèle à la frontière, chaque branche l'indique
Un tournant va surgir, prompt comme une fumée
Où flottera bonjour arqué comme une écharde
L'angoisse de faiblir sous l'écorce respire
Le couvert sera mis autour de la margelle
Des êtres bienveillants se porteront vers nous
La main à votre front sera froide d'étoiles
Et pas un souvenir de couteau sur les herbes

Non, le bruit de l'oubli serait tel
Qu'il corromprait la vertu du sang et de la cendre
Ligués à mon chevet contre la pauvreté
Qui n'entend que son pas n'admire que sa vue
Dans l'eau morte de son ombre.

Remittance

Let the reins go now, it's the plain
It freezes at the border, each branch signals it
A turning is on the point of appearing, quick like a smoke
Where hello will hesitate arched like a splinter
The anguish of weakening breathes under the bark
The table will be set around the well's rim
Benevolent beings will draw near us
The hand on your forehead will be cold with stars
And not one memory of a knife on the grasses

Now the noise of oblivion there would suffice
To corrupt the virtue of blood and of ashes
Bound together at my bed against poverty
Hearing only its step you admire only its aspect
In the stagnant water of its shadow.

M.A.C.

43

FUREUR ET MYSTERE

1938-1947

FUROR AND MYSTERY

1938-1947

L'homme fuit l'asphyxie.

L'homme dont l'appétit hors de l'imagination se calfeutre sans finir de s'approvisionner, se délivrera par les mains, rivières soudainement grossies.

L'homme qui s'époexpointe dans la prémonition, qui déboise son silence intérieur et le répartit en théâtres, ce second c'est le faiseur de pain.

Aux uns la prison et la mort. Aux autres la transhumance du Verbe.

Déborder l'économie de la création, agrandir le sang des gestes, devoir de toute lumière.

Nous tenons l'anneau où sont enchaînés côte à côte, d'une part le rossignol diabolique, d'autre part la clé angélique.

Sur les arêtes de notre amertume, l'aurore de la conscience s'avance et dépose son limon.

Aoûtement. Une dimension franchit le fruit de l'autre. Dimensions adversaires. Déporté de l'attelage et des noces, je bats le fer des fermoirs invisibles.

Man flees suffocation.

Man, whose appetite beyond imagination becomes airtight still laying in supplies, will find freedom by his hands, rivers suddenly swollen.

Man who grows blunt through premonitions, who deforests his inner silence and divides it into stages, the latter one is the maker of bread.

To the former, prison and death. To the latter, the repasturing of the Word.

To exceed the economy of creation, to increase the blood of gestures, task of all light.

We hold the ring where the devilish nightingale and the angelic key are chained together, side by side.

Over the ridge of our bitterness, the dawn of conscience advances and lays down its loam.

August ripening. One dimension traverses the fruit of the other. Warring dimensions. Deported from the yoke and from the nuptials, I strike the iron of invisible hinges.

M.A.C.

Vous qui m'avez connu, grenade dissidente, point du jour déployant le plaisir comme exemple, votre visage,—tel est-il, qu'il soit toujours,—si libre qu'à son contact le cerne infini de l'air se plissait, s'entr'ouvrant à ma rencontre, me vêtait des beaux quartiers de votre imagination. Je demeurais là, entièrement inconnu de moi-même, dans votre moulin à soleil, exultant à la succession des richesses d'un cœur qui avait rompu son étau. Sur notre plaisir s'allongeait l'influente douceur de la grande roue consumable du mouvement, au terme de ses classes.

A ce visage,—personne ne l'aperçut jamais,—simplifier la beauté n'apparaissait pas comme une atroce économie. Nous étions exacts dans l'exceptionnel qui seul sait se soustraire au caractère alternatif du mystère de vivre.

Dès lors que les routes de la mémoire se sont couvertes de la lèpre infaillible des monstres, je trouve refuge dans une innocence où l'homme qui rêve ne peut vieillir. Mais ai-je qualité pour m'imposer de vous survivre, moi qui dans ce Chant de Vous me considère comme le plus éloigné de mes sosies?

Bewitchment at the Renardière

You who have known me, dissentient pomegranate, day-break unfurling joy for an example, your face—as it is, may it always be—so free that at its touch air's infinite ring crumpled, half-opening as I met it, clothing me with the fine streets of your imagination. I remained there, entirely unknown to myself, in your sun mill, exulting at the successive riches of a heart which had snapped open its vice. Over our joy there stretched out the influential gentleness of motion's great consumable wheel, at the end of its classes.

For this face—no one ever perceived it—to simplify beauty never seemed an atrocious saving. We were exact in the exceptional, alone exempt from the alternate nature of the mystery of living.

Since memory's roads have cloaked themselves in the unfailing leprosy of monsters, I have found refuge in an innocence where the man who dreams cannot grow old. But am I the one to assume the task of surviving you, I who in this Song of You find myself the most distant of my counterparts?

M.A.C.

Le loriot

3 septembre 1939

Le loriot entra dans la capitale de l'aube.
L'épée de son chant ferma le lit triste.
Tout à jamais prit fin.

The Oriole

September 3, 1939

The oriole entered the capital of dawn.
The sword of his song closed the sad bed.
Everything forever ended.

M.A.C.

L'Absent

Ce frère brutal mais dont la parole était sûre, patient au sacrifice, diamant et sanglier, ingénieux et secourable, se tenait au centre de tous les malentendus tel un arbre de résine dans le froid inalliable. Au bestiaire de mensonges qui le tourmentait de ses gobelins et de ses trombes il opposait son dos perdu dans le temps. Il venait à vous par des sentiers invisibles, favorisait l'audace écarlate, ne vous contrariait pas, savait sourire. Comme l'abeille quitte le verger pour le fruit déjà noir, les femmes soutenaient sans le trahir le paradoxe de ce visage qui n'avait pas des traits d'otage.

J'ai essayé de vous décrire ce compère indélébile que nous sommes quelques-uns à avoir fréquenté. Nous dormirons dans l'espérance, nous dormirons en son absence, puisque la raison ne soupçonne pas que ce qu'elle nomme, à la légère, absence, occupe le fourneau dans l'unité.

The Absent one

This brutal brother but whose word was true, steadfast in the face of sacrifice, diamond and wild boar, ingenious and helpful, held himself in the center of all misunderstandings like a resinous tree in the cold admitting of no alloy. Against the bestiary of lies tormenting him with its goblins and its waterspouts, he set his back, lost in time. He came to you by invisible paths, preferred a scarlet forwardness, did not thwart you, knew how to smile. As the bee leaves the orchard for the fruit already black, women withstood without betraying it the paradox of this face which had none of the lineaments of a hostage.

I have tried to describe for you this indelible companion whose friendship some of us have kept. We shall sleep in hope, we shall sleep in his absence, reason not suspecting that what it names, thoughtlessly, absence, dwells within the crucible of unity.

M.A.C.

L'épi de cristal égrène dans les herbes sa moisson transparente

La ville n'était pas défaite. Dans la chambre devenue légère le donneur de liberté couvrait son amour de cet immense effort du corps, semblable à celui de la création d'un fluide par le jour. L'alchimie du désir rendait essentiel leur génie récent à l'univers de ce matin. Loin derrière eux leur mère ne les trahirait plus, leur mère si immobile. Maintenant ils précédaient le pays de leur avenir qui ne contenait encore que la flèche de leur bouche dont le chant venait de naître. Leur avidité rencontrait immédiatement son objet. Ils douaient d'omniprésence un temps qu'on n'interrogeait pas.

Il lui disait comment jadis dans des forêts persécutées il interpellait les animaux auxquels il apportait leur chance, son serment aux monts internés qui l'avait conduit à la reconnaissance de son exemplaire destin et quel boucher secret il avait dû vaincre pour acquérir à ses yeux la tolérance de son semblable.

Dans la chambre devenue légère et qui peu à peu développait les grands espaces du voyage, le donneur de liberté s'apprêtait à disparaître, à se confondre avec d'autres naissances, une nouvelle fois.

The Crystal Wheat-ear Sheds in the Grasses its Transparent Harvest

The town was not undone. In the room become weightless, the bestower of freedom covered his beloved with this immense bodily effort, akin to a fluid's creation by the day. Desire in its alchemy rendered essential their recent genius to that morning's universe. Far behind them, their mother would betray them no more, their mother so unmoving. Now they preceded the country of their future which contained as yet only the arrow of their mouth whose song had just been born. Their avidity met its object straightaway. They endowed with omnipresence a time free of questioning.

He told her how in days gone by, in the persecuted forests, he would summon animals to whom he brought their chance, how his oath to the imprisoned mountains had made him recognize his exemplary fate and what secret butcher he'd had to conquer before winning in his own eyes his fellow-man's tolerance.

In the room become weightless and gradually unfurling vast expanses of voyage, the bestower of freedom readied himself to disappear, to mingle with other births, once again.

M.A.C.

Louis Curel de la Sorgue

Sorgue qui t'avances derrière un rideau de papillons qui pétillent, ta faucille de doyen loyal à la main, la crémaillère du supplice en collier à ton cou, pour accomplir ta journée d'homme, quand pourrai-je m'éveiller et me sentir heureux au rythme modelé de ton seigle irréprochable? Le sang et la sueur ont engagé leur combat qui se poursuivra jusqu'au soir, jusqu'à ton retour, solitude aux marges de plus en plus grandes. L'arme de tes maîtres, l'horloge des marées, achève de pourrir. La création et la risée se dissocient. L'air-roi s'annonce. Sorgue, tes épaules comme un livre ouvert propagent leur lecture. Tu as été, enfant, le fiancé de cette fleur au chemin tracé dans le rocher, qui s'évadait par un frelon . . . Courbé, tu observes aujourd'hui l'agonie du persécuteur qui arracha à l'aimant de la terre la cruauté d'innombrables fourmis pour la jeter en millions de meurtriers contre les tiens et ton espoir. Écrase donc encore une fois cet œuf cancéreux qui résiste . . .

Il y a un homme à présent debout, un homme dans un champ de seigle, un champ pareil à un chœur mitraillé, un champ sauvé.

Louis Curel de la Sorgue[3]

Sorgue advancing behind a curtain of flickering butterflies, holding your sickle of loyal elder, the torture rack worn as a necklace, to fulfill your man-long day, when may I waken joyous at the graven rhythm of your irreproachable rye? Blood and sweat have joined their combat which will last until evening, until your return, solitude with ever greater margins. All but rotted now, the weapon of your master, the clock of tides. Creation and mockery separate. The air-king proclaims his coming. Sorgue, your shoulders propagate their reading like an open book. As a child, you were betrothed to the flower whose path was traced in rock, who escaped by a hornet. . . . Stooping, you observe today the agony of the persecutor who wrenched from the terrestrial magnet the cruelty of innumerable ants to hurl it in murderous millions against your people and your hope. Crush then once more this cancerous egg resisting. . . .

There is a man now standing, a man in a field of rye, a field like a machine-gunned chorus, a field redeemed.

M.A.C.

---

[3] Sorgue: the river that springs from the Fontaine de Vaucluse and flows into the river Rhone at Avignon. The poet's native town, L'Isle-sur-la-Sorgue, set in a fertile plain midway between those points, remained, up to the nineteenth century, a town of fishermen making their living from the river. By the title "de la Sorgue," the poet confers on Louis Curel a natural nobility, in an intuitive convergence with a tradition. For, as he discovered years later, in the archives of the town there can be found the records of the election, around 1450, of a king of the fishermen, "Rex fluminis Sorgae," named by his peers "pour l'utilité du fleuve." See also Char's play *Le Soleil des eaux* (Paris, Gallimard, 1951) about the Sorgue and its people.

Ne s'entend pas

Au cours de la lutte si noire et de l'immobilité si noire, la terreur aveuglant mon royaume, je m'élevai des lions ailés de la moisson jusqu'au cri froid de l'anémone. Je vins au monde dans la difformité des chaînes de chaque être. Nous nous faisions libres tous deux. Je tirai d'une morale compatible les secours irréprochables. Malgré la soif de disparaître, je fus prodigue dans l'attente, la foi vaillante. Sans renoncer.

Vivre avec de tels hommes

Tellement j'ai faim, je dors sous la canicule des preuves. J'ai voyagé jusqu'à l'épuisement, le front sur le séchoir noueux. Afin que le mal demeure sans relève, j'ai étouffé ses engagements. J'ai effacé son chiffre de la gaucherie de mon étrave. J'ai répliqué aux coups. On tuait de si près que le monde s'est voulu meilleur. Brumaire de mon âme jamais escaladé, qui fait feu dans la bergerie déserte? Ce n'est plus la volonté elliptique de la scrupuleuse solitude. Aile double des cris d'un million de crimes se levant soudain dans des yeux jadis négligents, montrez-nous vos desseins et cette large abdication du remords!

.   .   .   .

Montre-toi; nous n'en avions jamais fini avec le sublime bien-être des très maigres hirondelles. Avides de s'approcher de l'ample allégement. Incertains dans le temps que l'amour grandissait. Incertains, eux seuls, au sommet du cœur.
Tellement j'ai faim.

Unheard

During the battle so dark and the darkest immobility, terror blinding my kingdom, I rose from the winged lions of the harvest to the anemone's cold cry. I was born in the deformity of each being's bonds. We made one another free. From a compatible morality I drew irreproachable succor. Thirsting to disappear, I was nevertheless prodigal in waiting, my faith unshaken. No renunciation.

M.A.C.

To Live with such Men

So hungry am I that I sleep under the dog-days of proofs. I've traveled to exhaustion, my forehead pressed against the knotted drying-rack. Lest evil be perpetuated, I have stifled its commitments, removed its sign from the awkwardness of my bowsprit. I answered volley with volley. Killing came so near that the world willed itself a better one. Brumaire of my soul, never scaled, who is firing in the deserted sheep pen? No longer is it the elliptical desire of a scrupulous solitude. Double wing of cries of a million crimes looming up suddenly in eyes once negligent, show us your purpose and this wide abdication from remorse!

. . . .

Show us your presence, we had not done with the sublime well-being of the thinnest swallows. Avid to move toward an ample assuaging. Irresolute within the time of love's growing. Irresolute, they only, at the heart's summit. So hungry am I.

M.A.C.

59

Chant du refus
Début du partisan

Le poète est retourné pour de longues années dans le néant du père. Ne l'appelez pas, vous tous qui l'aimez. S'il vous semble que l'aile de l'hirondelle n'a plus de miroir sur terre, oubliez ce bonheur. Celui qui panifiait la souffrance n'est pas visible dans sa léthargie rougeoyante.

Ah! beauté et vérité fassent que vous soyez *présents* nombreux aux salves de la délivrance!

Carte du 8 novembre

Les clous dans notre poitrine, la cécité transissant nos os, qui s'offre à les subjuguer? Pionniers de la vieille église, affluence du Christ, vous occupez moins de place dans la prison de notre douleur que le trait d'un oiseau sur la corniche de l'air. La foi! Son baiser s'est détourné avec horreur de ce nouveau calvaire. Comment son bras tiendrait-il démurée notre tête, lui qui vit, retranché des fruits de son prochain, de la charité d'une serrure inexacte? Le suprême écœurement, celui à qui la mort même refuse son ultime fumée, se retire, déguisé en seigneur.

Notre maison vieillira à l'écart de nous, épargnant le souvenir de notre amour couché intact dans la tranchée de sa seule reconnaissance.

Tribunal implicite, cyclone vulnéraire, que tu nous rends tard le but et la table où la faim entrait la première! Je suis aujourd'hui pareil à un chien enragé enchaîné à un arbre plein de rires et de feuilles.

60

Refusal Song
Beginning of the Partisan

The poet has returned for a long span of years into the naught of the father. Do not call him, all you who love him. If it seems to you that the swallow's wing has no longer a mirror on earth, forget that happiness. He who worked suffering into bread is not visible in his glowing lethargy.

Ah! may beauty and truth ensure your numerous *presence* at the salvos of liberation!

M.A.C.

Map of November 8

The nails piercing our breast, the blindness chilling our bones, who volunteers to subjugate them? Pioneers of the old church, multitude of Christ, you take less space in our pain's prison than a bird-streak on the cornice of air. Faith! Its kiss has turned away horrified from this new calvary. How should its arm maintain our head unwalled, this arm living at a remove from its neighbor's fruits, on the charity of an ill-fitting lock? Supreme loathing, refused the last smoke of death itself, draws back, in lordly disguise.

Our house will age apart from us, sparing the memory of our love laid intact in the trench of its sole gratitude.

Implicit tribunal, healing cyclone, how late you restore to us the aim and the table where hunger entered first! Today I am like a mad dog chained to a tree full of laughter and of leaves.

M.A.C.

61

Hommage et famine

Femme qui vous accordez avec la bouche du poète, ce torrent au limon serein, qui lui avez appris, alors qu'il n'était encore qu'une graine captive de loup anxieux, la tendresse des hauts murs polis par votre nom (hectares de Paris, entrailles de beauté, mon feu monte sous vos robes de fugue), Femme qui dormez dans le pollen des fleurs, déposez sur son orgueil votre givre de médium illimité, afin qu'il demeure jusqu'à l'heure de la bruyère d'ossements l'homme qui pour mieux vous adorer reculait indéfiniment en vous la diane de sa naissance, le poing de sa douleur, l'horizon de sa victoire.

(Il faisait nuit. Nous nous étions serrés sous le grand chêne de larmes. Le grillon chanta. Comment savait-il, solitaire, que la terre n'allait pas mourir, que nous, les enfants sans clarté, allions bientôt parler?)

La liberté

Elle est venue par cette ligne blanche pouvant tout aussi bien signifier l'issue de l'aube que le bougeoir du crépuscule.

Elle passa les grèves machinales; elle passa les cimes éventrées.

Prenaient fin la renonciation à visage de lâche, la sainteté du mensonge, l'alcool du bourreau.

Son verbe ne fut pas un aveugle bélier mais la toile où s'inscrivit mon souffle.

D'un pas à ne se mal guider que derrière l'absence, elle est venue, cygne sur la blessure, par cette ligne blanche.

62

Homage and Famine

Woman tuned to the mouth of the poet, this torrent with serene alluvium, who taught him when he was only a captive seed of anxious wolf, the tenderness of high walls burnished by your name (acres of Paris, entrails of beauty, my fire rises under your dresses of fugue), Woman sleeping in flower pollen, lay lightly on his pride your frost of limitless medium, that he remain until the hour of the heather of bones the man who the better to adore you thrust back unendingly in you the clarion of his birth, the fist of his suffering, the horizon of his victory.

(It was night. We were huddled under the great oak of tears. The cricket chirped. How did he know, solitary, that the earth was not to die, that we, children without clarity, were soon to speak?)

M.A.C.

Freedom

It came along this white line that might signify dawn's emergence as well as dusk's candlestick.

It passed beyond the unconscious strands; it passed beyond the eviscerated summits.

They were ending: the cowardly-countenanced renunciation, the holiness of lying, the raw spirits of the executioner.

Its word was not a blind battering-ram but rather the canvas where my breath was inscribed.

With a pace unsure only behind absence, it came, a swan on the wound, along this white line.

M.A.C.

63

Conduite

Passe.
La bêche sidérale
autrefois là s'est engouffrée.
Ce soir un village d'oiseaux
très haut exulte et passe.

Écoute aux tempes rocheuses
des présences dispersées
le mot qui fera ton sommeil
chaud comme un arbre de septembre.

Vois bouger l'entrelacement
des certitudes arrivées
près de nous à leur quintessence,
ô ma Fourche, ma Soif anxieuse!

La rigueur de vivre se rode
sans cesse à convoiter l'exil.
Par une fine pluie d'amande
mêlée de liberté docile,
ta gardienne alchimie s'est produite,
ô Bien-aimée!

Convey

Pass.
The sidereal spade
Long ago struck in there.
Tonight a high village of birds
Exults and passes.

Listen at the stony temples
of presences dispersed
to the word making your sleep
warm as a September tree.

Mark the moving of the interwoven certainties
that beside us have attained
their quintessence,
oh my Cleaving, my anxious Thirst!

The rigor of living ceaselessly
Wears down, coveting exile.
Through a fine rain of almond
mingled with gentle liberty,
your guardian alchemy has done its work,
oh Beloved!

M.A.C.

A présent disparais, mon escorte, debout dans la distance;
La douceur du nombre vient de se détruire.
Congé à vous, mes alliés, mes violents, mes indices.
Tout vous entraîne, tristesse obséquieuse.
J'aime.
L'eau est lourde à un jour de la source.
La parcelle vermeille franchit ses lentes branches à ton
front, dimension rassurée.
Et moi semblable à toi,
Avec la paille en fleur au bord du ciel criant ton nom,
J'abats les vestiges,
Atteint, sain de clarté.

Ceinture de vapeur, multitude assouplie, diviseurs de la
crainte, touchez ma renaissance.
Parois de ma durée, je renonce à l'assistance de ma largeur
vénielle;
Je boise l'expédient du gîte, j'entrave la primeur des sur-
vies.
Embrasé de solitude foraine,
J'évoque la nage sur l'ombre de sa Présence.

Le corps désert, hostile à son mélange, hier était revenu
parlant noir.
Déclin, ne te ravise pas, tombe ta massue de transes, aigre
sommeil.
Le décolleté diminue les ossements de ton exil, de ton
escrime;
Tu rends fraîche la servitude qui se dévore le dos;
Risée de la nuit, arrête ce charroi lugubre
De voix vitreuses, de départs lapidés.

The Nuptial Countenance

Now let my escort disappear, standing far off into the
     distance;
Numbers have just lost their sweetness.
I give you leave, my allies, my violent ones, my indices.
Everything summons you away, fawning sorrow.
I am in love.

Water is heavy at a day's flow from the spring.
The crimson foliage traverses its slow branches at your
     forehead, dimension reassured.
And I, like you,
With the straw in flower at the edge of the sky crying your
     name,
I cut down the traces,
Stricken, strong in clarity.

Ring of vapor, many made supple, dividers of fear, touch
     my renewal.
Walls of my enduring, I renounce the succor of my venial
     breadth;
I timber the device of the dwelling, I thwart the first-fruits
     of survivals.
Afire with itinerant solitude,
I invoke the swimming on the shade of her Presence.

The desert body hostile to an alloyage, had returned yes-
     terday, speaking darkly.
Decline, do not halt your movement, let fall your blud-
     geon of seizures, acrid sleep.
Indentation diminishes the bones of your exile, of your
     sparring;
You freshen constraint self-devouring
Gust of the night, halt this grim cartage
Of glazed voices, departures pelted with stones.

Tôt soustrait au flux des lésions inventives
(La pioche de l'aigle lance haut le sang évasé)
Sur un destin présent j'ai mené mes franchises
Vers l'azur multivalve, la granitique dissidence.

O voûte d'effusion sur la couronne de son ventre,
Murmure de dot noire!
O mouvement tari de sa diction!
Nativité, guidez les insoumis, qu'ils découvrent leur base,
L'amande croyable au lendemain neuf.
Le soir a fermé sa plaie de corsaire où voyageaient les
    fusées vagues parmi la peur soutenue des chiens.
Au passé les micas du deuil sur ton visage.

Vitre inextinguible: mon souffle affleurait déjà l'amitié
    de ta blessure,
Armait ta royauté inapparente.
Et des lèvres du brouillard descendit notre plaisir au seuil
    de dune, au toit d'acier.
La conscience augmentait l'appareil frémissant de ta per-
    manence;
La simplicité fidèle s'étendit partout.

Timbre de la devise matinale, morte-saison de l'étoile
    précoce,
Je cours au terme de mon cintre, colisée fossoyé.
Assez baisé le crin nubile des céréales:
La cardeuse, l'opiniâtre, nos confins la soumettent.
Assez maudit le havre des simulacres nuptiaux:
Je touche le fond d'un retour compact.

Soon subtracted from the flux of contriving lesions
(The eagle's pickaxe flings high the flaring blood)
Across a present destiny I have led my exemptions
Toward an azure multivalved, granite dissidence.

Oh vaulted effusion upon the crown of her belly,
Murmurings of dark dowry!
Oh the exhausted motion of her diction!
Nativity, guide the unyielding, may they find their
    foundations,
The almond believable in the fresh day to come.
Evening has closed its corsair's gash where the rockets
    soared aimlessly amid a dogged fear.
Past now the micas of mourning on your face.

Unquenchable pane: my breath was already grazing the
    friendship of your wound,
Arming your hidden royalty.
And from the lips of the fog descended our joy with its
    threshold of dune, its roof of steel.
Awareness increased the quivering array of your per-
    manence;
Faithful simplicity spread everywhere.

Tone of morning's adage, slack season of the precocious
    star,
I rush to the term of my arch, interred coliseum.
Long enough embraced, the nubile hair of grain:
Oh stubborn one, carder, our reaches force its submission.
Long enough condemned, the haven of nuptial sem-
    blances:
I touch the depths of a compact return.

Ruisseaux, neume des morts anfractueux,
Vous qui suivez le ciel aride,
Mêlez votre acheminement aux orages de qui sut guérir
de la désertion,
Donnant contre vos études salubres.
Au sein du toit le pain suffoque à porter cœur et lueur.
Prends, ma Pensée, la fleur de ma main pénétrable,
Sens s'éveiller l'obscure plantation.

Je ne verrai pas tes flancs, ces essaims de faim, se des-
sécher, s'emplir de ronces;
Je ne verrai pas l'empuse te succéder dans ta serre;
Je ne verrai pas l'approche des baladins inquiéter le jour
renaissant;
Je ne verrai pas la race de notre liberté servilement se
suffire.

Chimères, nous sommes montés au plateau.
Le silex frissonnait sous les sarments de l'espace;
La parole, lasse de défoncer, buvait au débarcadère angé-
lique.
Nulle farouche survivance:
L'horizon des routes jusqu'à l'afflux de rosée,
L'intime dénouement de l'irréparable.

Voici le sable mort, voici le corps sauvé:
La Femme respire, l'Homme se tient debout.

Streams, neuma of the craggy dead,
You who follow the arid sky,
Mingle your going with his tempests, who could heal
    desertion,
Striking against your saving studies.
At the roof's center bread suffocates carrying heart and
    light.
Take, oh my Thought, the flower of my penetrable hand.
Feel the dark planting waken.

I shall not see your sides, those swarms of hunger, dry
    up, be overrun with brambles;
I shall not see the mantis replace you in your greenhouse;
I shall not see the minstrels approach, disquieting the
    reborn day;
I shall not see our freedom's lineage servile in self-
    sufficiency.

Chimeras, we have climbed upland
The flint was quivering under the vine-shoots of space;
The word, tired of battering, drank at the angelic wharf.
No savage survival:
The horizon of roads until the abounding dew,
Intimate unfolding of the irreparable.

This is the sand dead, this the body saved:
Woman breathes, Man stands upright.

M.A.C.

Evadné

L'été et notre vie étions d'un seul tenant
La campagne mangeait la couleur de ta jupe odorante
Avidité et contrainte s'étaient réconciliées
Le château de Maubec s'enfonçait dans l'argile
Bientôt s'effondrerait le roulis de sa lyre
La violence des plantes nous faisait vaciller
Un corbeau rameur sombre déviant de l'escadre
Sur le muet silex de midi écartelé
Accompagnait notre entente aux mouvements tendres
La faucille partout devait se reposer
Notre rareté commençait un règne
(Le vent insomnieux qui nous ride la paupière
En tournant chaque nuit la page consentie
Veut que chaque part de toi que je retienne
Soit étendue à un pays d'âge affamé et de larmier géant)

C'était au début d'adorables années
La terre nous aimait un peu je me souviens.

Evadne

We were summer and our life of a single tenant
The landscape devoured the color of your sweet-smelling
   skirt
Avidity and constraint had been reconciled
The château of Maubec was settling in the clay
Soon the rolling of its lyre would cease
The violence of plants made us reel
A crow, somber rower swerving from the fleet,
On the mute flint of quartered noon
Accompanied our understanding with tender movements
Everywhere the sickle must have been at rest
Our rarity was opening a reign
(The sleepless wind rippling our eyelids
Turning each night the page consented
Wishes any part of you that I retain
Might extend to a country of famished age and high
   tear-stone)

This was at the outset of adorable years
The earth loved us a little I remember.

M.A.C.

Post-scriptum

Écartez-vous de moi qui patiente sans bouche;
A vos pieds je suis né, mais vous m'avez perdu;
Mes feux ont trop précisé leur royaume;
Mon trésor a coulé contre votre billot.

Le désert comme asile au seul tison suave
Jamais ne m'a nommé, jamais ne m'a rendu.

Écartez-vous de moi qui patiente sans bouche:
Le trèfle de la passion est de fer dans ma main.

Dans la stupeur de l'air où s'ouvrent mes allées,
Le temps émondera peu à peu mon visage,
Comme un cheval sans fin dans un labour aigri.

Post-scriptum

Go from me now in my mouthless waiting;
At your feet I was born, but you have lost me;
My desires have made their kingdom too precise;
Against your block my treasure has run out.

The desert as refuge of the sole sweet fire-brand
Named me never, never restored me.

Go from me now in my mouthless waiting;
Passion's trefoil is iron in my hand.

In the air's amazement where my ventures open,
Time will prune away my visage, bit by bit,
Like a horse ceaseless in an embittered ploughing.

M.A.C.

Le Thor

Dans le sentier aux herbes engourdies où nous nous étonnions, enfants, que la nuit se risquât à passer, les guêpes n'allaient plus aux ronces et les oiseaux aux branches. L'air ouvrait aux hôtes de la matinée sa turbulente immensité. Ce n'étaient que filaments d'ailes, tentation de crier, voltige entre lumière et transparence. Le Thor s'exaltait sur la lyre de ses pierres. Le mont Ventoux, miroir des aigles, était en vue.

Dans le sentier aux herbes engourdies, la chimère d'un âge perdu souriait à nos jeunes larmes.

Le Thor[4]

In the path of benumbed grasses where we, as children, wondered that night ventured to pass, wasps went no more to brambles, nor birds to branches. Air opened to the morning guests its turbulent boundlessness. Everywhere, filaments of wings, temptation to cry aloud, vaulting between light and transparency. Le Thor exalted itself on its lyre of stones. The Ventoux, mirror of eagles, was in sight.

In the path of benumbed grasses, the chimera of a lost age smiled at our young tears.

M.A.C.

[4] Le Thor is a small town also watered by the Sorgue, lying in the plain at the foot of the Monts du Vaucluse. The Mont Ventoux looms to the north, a lone bare height.

Pénombre

J'étais dans une de ces forêts où le soleil n'a pas accès mais où, la nuit, les étoiles pénètrent. Ce lieu n'avait le permis d'exister, que parce que l'inquisition des états l'avait négligé. Les servitudes abandonnées me marquaient leur mépris. La hantise de punir m'était retirée. Par endroit, le souvenir d'une force caressait la fugue paysanne de l'herbe. Je me gouvernais sans doctrine, avec une véhémence sereine. J'étais l'égal de choses dont le secret tenait sous le rayon d'une aile. Pour la plupart, l'essentiel n'est jamais né, et ceux qui le possèdent ne peuvent l'échanger sans se nuire. Nul ne consent à perdre ce qu'il a conquis à la pointe de sa peine! Autrement ce serait la jeunesse et la grâce, source et delta auraient la même pureté.

J'étais dans une de ces forêts où le soleil n'a pas accès mais où, la nuit, les étoiles pénètrent pour d'implacables hostilités.

Cette fumée qui nous portait ...

Cette fumée qui nous portait était sœur du bâton qui dérange la pierre et du nuage qui ouvre le ciel. Elle n'avait pas mépris de nous, nous prenait tels que nous étions, minces ruisseaux nourris de désarroi et d'espérance, avec un verrou aux mâchoires et une montagne dans le regard.

Penumbra

I was in one of those forests to which the sun has no access, but where stars penetrate by night. This place was allowed existence only because the inquisition of the State had overlooked it. Forsaken easements showed me their scorn. The obsession to chastise was taken from me. Here and there, the memory of a strength caressed the peasant flights of the grass. I ruled myself without doctrine, in serene vehemence. I was the equal of things whose secret fitted under the beam of a wing. For most, the essential is never born, and its possessors cannot exchange it without harm to themselves. None consents to lose what he has conquered by dint of his pain! Otherwise, it would be youth and grace, spring and delta would have the same purity.

I was in one of those forests to which the sun has no access, but where stars penetrate by night for a relentless warring.

M.A.C.

This Smoke which Bore Us

This smoke which bore us was sister to the rod disturbing the rock and to the cloud opening the sky. It did not scorn us, took us as we were, narrow rivulets nourished on confusion and hope, with a bolt to our jaws and a mountain in our gaze.

M.A.C.

Cur secessisti?

Neige, caprice d'enfant, soleil qui n'as que l'hiver pour devenir un astre, au seuil de mon cachot de pierre, venez vous abriter. Sur les pentes d'Aulan, mes fils qui sont incendiaires, mes fils qu'on tue sans leur fermer les yeux, s'augmentent de votre puissance.

Cur Secessisti?

Snow, a child's fancy, sun that has only winter to become a star, on the threshold of my stone dungeon come and shelter. On the slopes of Aulan my sons who are fire-raisers, my sons whom men kill without closing their eyes for them, gain increase from your power.

J.G.

81

Redonnez-leur . . .

Redonnez-leur ce qui n'est plus présent en eux,
Ils reverront le grain de la moisson s'enfermer dans
  l'épi et s'agiter sur l'herbe.
Apprenez-leur, de la chute à l'essor, les douze mois de
  leur visage,
Ils chériront le vide de leur cœur jusqu'au désir suivant;
Car rien ne fait naufrage ou ne se plaît aux cendres;
Et qui sait voir la terre aboutir à des fruits,
Point ne l'émeut l'échec quoiqu'il ait tout perdu.

82

Restore to them what is no more present in them,
They shall see again the harvest grain shelter in the ear
    and sway on the stalk.
Teach them, from fall to soaring, the twelve months of
    their face,
They shall cherish their heart's emptiness until the next
    desire;
For nothing suffers shipwreck or contents itself in the
    cinders;
And a man who can watch the earth through to its end
    in fruit—
Failure does not shake him though he has lost all.

                                                            J.G.

Fastes

L'été chantait sur son roc préféré quand tu m'es apparue, l'été chantait à l'écart de nous qui étions silence, sympathie, liberté triste, mer plus encore que la mer dont la longue pelle bleue s'amusait à nos pieds.

L'été chantait et ton cœur nageait loin de lui. Je baisais ton courage, entendais ton désarroi. Route par l'absolu des vagues vers ces hauts pics d'écume où croisent des vertus meurtrières pour les mains qui portent nos maisons. Nous n'étions pas crédules. Nous étions entourés.

Les ans passèrent. Les orages moururent. Le monde s'en alla. J'avais mal de sentir que ton cœur justement ne m'apercevait plus. Je t'aimais. En mon absence de visage et mon vide de bonheur. Je t'aimais, changeant en tout, fidèle à toi.

Annals[5]

Summer was singing on its favorite rock when you appeared to me, summer was singing apart as we who were silence, sympathy, sorrowful freedom, were sea still more than the sea whose long blue spade was playing at our feet.

Summer was singing and your heart swam far from it. I embraced your courage, heard your confusion. Road along the absolute of waves toward those high peaks of foam where virtues sail, murderous to hands bearing our houses. We were not credulous. We were surrounded.

The years passed by. The storms died down. The world went its way. I suffered to think it was your heart which no longer perceived me. I loved you. In my absence of visage and my emptiness of joy. I loved you, changing in every way, faithful to you.

M.A.C.

[5] Into the plural "Fastes" or the annals of memorable events, inscribed on marble tablets in Roman times (as in Ovid's *Fasti*), there enters also a trace of the singular "faste" or display.

Nous regardions couler devant nous l'eau grandissante. Elle effaçait d'un coup la montagne, se chassant de ses flancs maternels. Ce n'était pas un torrent qui s'offrait à son destin mais une bête ineffable dont nous devenions la parole et la substance. Elle nous tenait amoureux sur l'arc tout-puissant de son imagination. Quelle intervention eût pu nous contraindre? La modicité quotidienne avait fui, le sang jeté était rendu à sa chaleur. Adoptés par l'ouvert, poncés jusqu'à l'invisible, nous étions une victoire qui ne prendrait jamais fin.

The First Moments

We were watching the water as it flowed, increasing before us. It effaced the mountain suddenly, expelling itself from her maternal side. Not a torrent submitting to its fate but an ineffable beast whose word and substance we became. It held us amorous on the all-powerful arch of its imagination. What intervention could have constrained us? Daily tameness had fled, blood cast aside was rendered to its heat. Adopted by the open, abraded to invisibility, we were a victory that would never end.

M.A.C.

Le martinet

Martinet aux ailes trop larges, qui vire et crie sa joie autour de la maison. Tel est le cœur.

Il dessèche le tonnerre. Il sème dans le ciel serein. S'il touche au sol, il se déchire.

Sa repartie est l'hirondelle. Il déteste la familière. Que vaut dentelle de la tour?

Sa pause est au creux le plus sombre. Nul n'est plus à l'étroit que lui.

L'été de la longue clarté, il filera dans les ténèbres, par les persiennes de minuit.

Il n'est pas d'yeux pour le tenir. Il crie, c'est toute sa présence. Un mince fusil va l'abattre. Tel est le cœur.

The Swift

Swift with wings too wide, wheeling and shrieking his joy around the house. Such is the heart.

He dries up thunder. He sows in the serene sky. If he touches ground, he tears himself apart.

His response is the swallow, the familiar, whom he detests. What value has lace from the tower?

His pause is in the most somber hollow. No one lives in space more narrow than he.

Through the summer of long brightness, he will streak his way in shadows, by the blinds of midnight.

No eyes can hold him. He shrieks for his only presence. A slight gun is about to fell him. Such is the heart.

M.A.C.

89

La Sorgue
Chanson pour Yvonne

Rivière trop tôt partie, d'une traite, sans compagnon,
Donne aux enfants de mon pays le visage de ta passion.

Rivière où l'éclair finit et où commence ma maison,
Qui roule aux marches d'oubli la rocaille de ma raison.

Rivière, en toi terre est frisson, soleil anxiété.
Que chaque pauvre dans sa nuit fasse son pain de ta
   moisson.

Rivière souvent punie, rivière à l'abandon.

Rivière des apprentis à la calleuse condition,
Il n'est vent qui ne fléchisse à la crête de tes sillons.

Rivière de l'âme vide, de la guenille et du soupçon,
Du vieux malheur qui se dévide, de l'ormeau, de la
   compassion.

Rivière des farfelus, des fiévreux, des équarrisseurs,
Du soleil lâchant sa charrue pour s'acoquiner au menteur.

Rivière des meilleurs que soi, rivière des brouillards éclos,
De la lampe qui désaltère l'angoisse autour de son
   chapeau.

Rivière des égards au songe, rivière qui rouille le fer,
Où les étoiles ont cette ombre qu'elles refusent à la mer.

Rivière des pouvoirs transmis et du cri embouquant les
   eaux,
De l'ouragan qui mord la vigne et annonce le vin nouveau.

Rivière au cœur jamais détruit dans ce monde fou de
   prison,
Garde-nous violent et ami des abeilles de l'horizon.

The Sorgue
Song for Yvonne

River, hasty starter, at a bound, with no companion,
Give the children of my country the features of your
  passion.

River where the lightning ends and my home rises,
Rolling to the steps of oblivion the rubble of my reason.

River, in you earth is shudder, sun unrest,
Let every poor man in his night make his bread of your
  harvest.

River often punished, river left to drift.

River of those apprenticed to the callousing condition,
Not a wind but bends at your furrows' crest.

River of the empty soul, of rags and of suspicion,
Of old trouble unwinding, of the elm, of compassion.

River of the fey, the fevered, the knacker in his yard,
The sun dropping his plough to hobnob with a liar.

River of men better than oneself, river of fog-blooms,
Of the lamp quenching dread in a circle round its hat.

River of respect for dreams, river that rusts iron,
Where the stars have the shadow they refuse to the sea.

River of powers transmitted, the cry essaying the waters,
The autumn gale that bites the vine and announces the
  new wine.

River with heart never destroyed in this world crazy for
  prison,
Keep us violent and a friend to the bees of the horizon.

                                                      J.G.

Madeleine à la veilleuse
par Georges de La Tour

Je voudrais aujourd'hui que l'herbe fût blanche pour fouler l'évidence de vous voir souffrir : je ne regarderais pas sous votre main si jeune la forme dure, sans crépi de la mort. Un jour discrétionnaire, d'autres pourtant moins avides que moi, retireront votre chemise de toile, occuperont votre alcôve. Mais ils oublieront en partant de noyer la veilleuse et un peu d'huile se répandra par le poignard de la flamme sur l'impossible solution.

Madeleine with the Vigil-lamp[6]
by Georges de La Tour

I would wish today that the grass were white to tread on
the proof of seeing you suffer: I'd not look under your hand,
so young, at death's hard form without rough-cast. One
discretionary day, others, though less avid than I, will
remove your homespun blouse, will occupy your alcove.
But they will forget to extinguish the lamp in their de-
parting and a little oil will spill out by the dagger of the
flame onto the impossible solution.

M.A.C.

---

[6] "Madeleine" and not "Magdalen" or "Mary-Magdalene" because
the poem, like de La Tour's painting, concerns the woman before her
sanctification.

Allégeance

Dans les rues de la ville il y a mon amour. Peu importe où il va dans le temps divisé. Il n'est plus mon amour, chacun peut lui parler. Il ne se souvient plus; qui au juste l'aima?

Il cherche son pareil dans le vœu des regards. L'espace qu'il parcourt est ma fidélité. Il dessine l'espoir et léger l'éconduit. Il est prépondérant sans qu'il y prenne part.

Je vis au fond de lui comme une épave heureuse. A son insu, ma solitude est son trésor. Dans le grand méridien où s'inscrit son essor, ma liberté le creuse.

Dans les rues de la ville il y a mon amour. Peu importe où il va dans le temps divisé. Il n'est plus mon amour, chacun peut lui parler. Il ne se souvient plus; qui au juste l'aima et l'éclaire de loin pour qu'il ne tombe pas?

Allegiance

In the streets of the town goes my love. Small matter where it moves in divided time. It is no longer my love, anyone may speak with it. It remembers no longer; who exactly loved it?

It seeks its equal in glances, pledging. The space it traverses is my faithfulness. It traces a hope and lightly dismisses it. It is dominant without taking part.

I live in its depth, a joyous shipwreck. Without its knowing, my solitude is its treasure. In the great meridian where its soaring inscribes itself, my freedom hollows out its place.

In the streets of the town goes my love. Small matter where it moves in divided time. It is no longer my love, anyone may speak with it. It remembers no longer; who exactly loved it and lights it from afar, lest it should fall?

M.A.C.

Argument

Comment vivre sans inconnu devant soi?

Les hommes d'aujourd'hui veulent que le poème soit à l'image de leur vie, faite de si peu d'égards, de si peu d'espace et brûlée d'intolérance.

Parce qu'il ne leur est plus loisible d'agir suprêmement, dans cette préoccupation fatale de se détruire par son semblable, parce que leur inerte richesse les freine et les enchaîne, les hommes d'aujourd'hui, l'instinct affaibli, perdent, tout en se gardant vivants, jusqu'à la poussière de leur nom.

Né de l'appel du devenir et de l'angoisse de la rétention, le poème, s'élevant de son puits de boue et d'étoiles, témoignera presque silencieusement, qu'il n'était rien en lui qui n'existât vraiment ailleurs, dans ce rebelle et solitaire monde des contradictions.

96

Argument

How can we live without the unknown in front of us?

Men of today want the poem to be in the image of their lives, composed of such little consideration, of such little space, and burned with intolerance.

Because it is no longer given to them to act supremely, in this fatal preoccupation of self-destruction at the hands of their fellow-men, because their inert wealth holds them back and enslaves them, men of today, their instinct weakened, lose—still keeping alive—even the dust of their names.

Born from the summons of becoming and from the anguish of retention, the poem, rising from its well of mud and of stars, will bear witness, almost silently, that it contained nothing which did not truly exist elsewhere, in this rebellious and solitary world of contradictions.

M.A.C.

Les trois sœurs

Mon amour à la robe de phare bleu,
je baise la fièvre de ton visage
où couche la lumière qui jouit en secret.

J'aime et je sanglote. Je suis vivant
et c'est ton cœur cette Étoile du Matin
à la durée victorieuse qui rougit avant
de rompre le combat des Constellations.

Hors de toi, que ma chair devienne la voile
qui répugne au vent.

I

Dans l'urne des temps secondaires
L'enfant à naître était de craie.
La marche fourchue des saisons
Abritait d'herbe l'inconnu.

La connaissance divisible
Pressait d'averses le printemps.
Un aromate de pays
Prolongeait la fleur apparue.

Communication qu'on outrage,
Écorce ou givre déposés;
L'air investit, le sang attise;
L'œil fait mystère du baiser.

Donnant vie à la route ouverte,
Le tourbillon vint aux genoux;
Et cet élan, le lit des larmes
S'en emplit d'un seul battement.

The Three Sisters

My love in the blue-beacon dress,
I kiss the fever of your face
where the light lies taking its secret joy.

I love and am sobbing. I am alive
and your heart is this Morning Star
with the victorious endurance blushing
before breaking the battle of Constellations.

Distant from you, may my body be the sail
shunning the wind.

I

In the urn of secondary times
The unborn child was of chalk.
The forked step of seasons
Sheltered the unknown with grass.

Knowledge divisible
Hastened springtime with torrents.
An aromatic of our land
Prolonged the visible flower.

Message we profane,
Bark or frost deposited;
Air besieges, blood inflames;
Eye makes a mystery of the kiss.

Giving life to the open road,
The whirlwind rose to the knees;
And from this stroke, the bed of tears
Fills up in a single thrust.

II

La seconde crie et s'évade
De l'abeille ambiante et du tilleul vermeil.
Elle est un jour de vent perpétuel,
Le dé bleu du combat, le guetteur qui sourit
Quand sa lyre profère: «Ce que je veux, sera.»

C'est l'heure de se taire
De devenir la tour
Que l'avenir convoite.

Le chasseur de soi fuit sa maison fragile:
Son gibier le suit n'ayant plus peur.

Leur clarté est si haute, leur santé si nouvelle,
Que ces deux qui s'en vont sans rien signifier
Ne sentent pas les sœurs les ramener à elles
D'un long bâillon de cendre aux forêts blanches.

III

Cet enfant sur ton épaule
Est ta chance et ton fardeau.
Terre en quoi l'orchidée brûle,
Ne le fatiguez pas de vous.

Restez fleur et frontière,
Restez manne et serpent;
Ce que la chimère accumule
Bientôt délaisse le refuge.

Meurent les yeux singuliers
Et la parole qui découvre.
La plaie qui rampe au miroir
Est maîtresse des deux bouges.

Violente l'épaule s'entr'ouvre;
Muet apparaît le volcan.
Terre sur quoi l'olivier brille,
Tout s'évanouit en passage.

II

The second cries out, escaping
From the ambient bee and the crimson lime.
She is a day of perpetual wind,
The blue die of battle, the watcher smiling
When his lyre speaks: "What I will, shall be."

It is the hour of keeping still,
Of becoming the tower
That the future covets.

The hunter of himself flees his fragile house:
His prey follows him no longer fearing.

So high in clarity, so fresh in being
That these two who depart meaning nothing
Do not sense the sisters retaining them
By a long gag of ashes in the white forests.

III

This child on your shoulder
Is your fortune and your burden
Land on which the orchid burns,
Don't make him weary of you.

Remain the frontier and the flower,
Remain the manna and the serpent;
What the chimera accumulates
Soon forsakes the refuge.

Let the singular eyes perish
And the word discovering.
The wound cringing in the mirror.
Is mistress of the two hovels.

Violent the shoulder parts asunder;
Mute the volcano appears.
Land where the olive tree glitters
All fades away in passage.

M.A.C.

101

Biens égaux

Je suis épris de ce morceau tendre de campagne, de son accoudoir de solitude au bord duquel les orages viennent se dénouer avec docilité, au mât duquel un visage perdu, par instant s'éclaire et me regagne. De si loin que je me souvienne, je me distingue penché sur les végétaux du jardin désordonné de mon père, attentif aux sèves, baisant des yeux formes et couleurs que le vent semi-nocturne irriguait mieux que la main infirme des hommes. Prestige d'un retour qu'aucune fortune n'offusque. Tribunaux de midi, je veille. Moi qui jouis du privilège de sentir tout ensemble accablement et confiance, défection et courage, je n'ai retenu personne sinon l'angle fusant d'une Rencontre.

Sur une route de lavande et de vin, nous avons marché côte à côte dans un cadre enfantin de poussière à gosier de ronces, l'un se sachant aimé de l'autre. Ce n'est pas un homme à tête de fable que plus tard tu baisais derrière les brumes de ton lit constant. Te voici nue et entre toutes la meilleure seulement aujourd'hui où tu franchis la sortie d'un hymne raboteux. L'espace pour toujours est-il cet absolu et scintillant congé, chétive volte-face? Mais prédisant cela j'affirme que tu vis; le sillon s'éclaire entre ton bien et mon mal. La chaleur reviendra avec le silence comme je te soulèverai, Inanimée.

Equal Goods

I am in love with this patch of countryside, with its railing of solitude at whose edge storms come gently undone, at whose mast a lost face lights up for an instant and wins me back again. From as long ago as I can remember, I see myself bent over the plants in my father's disorderly garden, attentive to the sap, embracing with my eyes the shapes and colours that the faintly nocturnal wind watered better than the feeble hand of man. Wonder of a return that no fortune offends. Law-courts of noontime, I keep watch. I who enjoy the privilege of feeling at once despondency and confidence, desertion and courage, I have retained no one save the fusing angle of an encounter.

On a road of lavender and wine, we walked side by side in a childlike setting of briar-throated dust, each knowing ourself loved by the other. It's not a man with a head of fiction whom you kissed later behind the mists of your constant bed. Here you are naked and the best of them all only today, when passing through the exit of a rough-hewn hymn. Is space for ever this absolute and sparkling departure, frail about-face? But in predicting that, I affirm your living; the furrow lights up between your good and my evil. Heat will return with silence as I shall lift you, Inanimate.

M.A.C.

J'habite une douleur

Ne laisse pas le soin de gouverner ton cœur à ces tendresses parentes de l'automne auquel elles empruntent sa placide allure et son affable agonie. L'œil est précoce à se plisser. La souffrance connaît peu de mots. Préfère te coucher sans fardeau: tu rêveras du lendemain et ton lit te sera léger. Tu rêveras que ta maison n'a plus de vitres. Tu es impatient de t'unir au vent, au vent qui parcourt une année en une nuit. D'autres chanteront l'incorporation mélodieuse, les chairs qui ne personnifient plus que la sorcellerie du sablier. Tu condamneras la gratitude qui se répète. Plus tard, on t'identifiera à quelque géant désagrégé, seigneur de l'impossible.

Pourtant.

Tu n'as fait qu'augmenter le poids de ta nuit. Tu es retourné à la pêche aux murailles, à la canicule sans été. Tu es furieux contre ton amour au centre d'une entente qui s'affole. Songe à la maison parfaite que tu ne verras jamais monter. A quand la récolte de l'abîme? Mais tu as crevé les yeux du lion. Tu crois voir passer la beauté au-dessus des lavandes noires . . .

Qu'est-ce qui t'a hissé, une fois encore, un peu plus haut, sans te convaincre?

Il n'y a pas de siège pur.

104

A Pain I Dwell In

Do not leave the task of governing your heart to those affections akin to autumn whose placid demeanor and whose affable death-pangs they borrow. Eyes are early in their narrowing. Suffering knows few words. Prefer to sleep unburdened: you will dream of the morrow and your bed will be light for you. You will dream that your house has window panes no longer. You are impatient to join with the wind, the wind rushing through a year in one night. Others will sing of the melodious embodying of substances, flesh personifying no longer other than an hourglass witchery. You will condemn gratitude repeating itself. Later they will identify you with some disaggregated giant, lord of the impossible.

However.

You have only increased the weight of your night. You have returned to high wall fishing,[7] to the dog-days with no summer. You are raging against your love at the center of a frenzied understanding. Think of the perfect house you will never see built. When shall it be, the harvest of the abyss? But you have put out the eyes of the lion. You think you see beauty passing above the black lavender. . . .

What has lifted you once again, slightly higher still, without convincing you?

There is no untainted seat.

M.A.C.

[7] Seen through the clear waters are the remains of a Roman wall. . . .

Seuil

Quand s'ébranla le barrage de l'homme,   ₁ faille
géante de l'abandon du divin, des mots   ₒintain,
des mots qui ne voulaient pas se perdre, ₒₙₐₑrent de ré-
sister à l'exorbitante poussée. Là se décida la dynastie de
leur sens.

J'ai couru jusqu'à l'issue de cette nuit diluvienne. Planté
dans le flageolant petit jour, ma ceinture pleine de saisons,
je vous attends, ô mes amis qui allez venir. Déjà je vous
devine derrière la noirceur de l'horizon. Mon âtre ne tarit
pas de vœux pour vos maisons. Et mon bâton de cyprès
rit de tout son cœur pour vous.

When the dam, which man is, shifted—breathed in by that giant crack, the abandonment of the divine—words in the distance, words that were refusing to be lost, tried to resist the exorbitant thrust. There the dynasty of their meaning was decided.

I have run to the outcome of this diluvian night. Taking my stand in the trembling dawn, with my belt full of seasons, I am waiting for you, my friends who will come. Already I divine you behind the black of the horizon. My hearth's good wishes for your homes never dry up. And my cypress walking-stick laughs with its whole heart for you.

J.G.

Il ne déplaçait pas d'ombre en avan   ne
audace tôt consumée, bien que son pa   ire.
Ceux qui, aux premières heures de la n   r lit
et le perdent ensuite de vue jusqu'au len   ivent
être tentés par les similitudes. Ils cherchent   .:e de
quelques pierres trop sages, trop chaudes, \ .ent se dé-
livrer de l'emprise des cristaux à prétention fabuleuse, que
la morne démarche du quotidien sécrète, aux lieux de son
choix, avec des attouchements de suaire. Tel n'était pas
ce marcheur que le voile du paysage lunaire, très bas,
semblait ne pas gêner dans son mouvement. Le gel furieux
effleurait la surface de son front sans paraître *personnel*.
Une route qui s'allonge, un sentier qui dévie sont con-
formes à l'élan de la pensée qui fredonne. Par la nuit
d'hiver fantastiquement propre parce qu'elle était com-
mune à la généralité des habitants de l'univers qui ne la
pénétraient pas, le dernier comédien n'allait plus exister.
Il avait perdu tout lien avec le volume ancien des sources
propices aux interrogations, avec les corps heureux qu'il
s'était plu à animer auprès du sien lorsqu'il pouvait en-
core assigner une cime à son plaisir, une neige à son talent.
Aujourd'hui il rompait avec la tristesse devenue un objet
aguerri, avec la frayeur du convenu. La terre avait faussé
sa persuasion, la terre, de sa vitesse un peu courte, avec
son imagination safranée, son usure crevassée par les actes
des monstres. Personne n'aurait à l'oublier car l'utile ne
l'avait pas assisté, ne l'avait pas dessiné en entier au re-
gard des autres. Sur le plafond de chaux blanche de sa
chambre, quelques oiseaux étaient passés mais leur éclair
avait fondu dans son sommeil.

Le voile du paysage lunaire maintenant très haut dé-
ploie ses couleurs aromatiques au-dessus du personnage
que je dis. Il sort éclairé du froid et tourne à jamais le dos
au printemps qui n'existe pas.

He displaced no shadow in his advance, betraying an audacity s oon burned out, although his step was rather commonplace. Those who miss their beds in the night's early hours and then lose sight of them until the morrow may be tempted by resemblances. They try to break away from stones too wise, too warm, wishing to escape from the hold of crystals of fabulous claim which daily usage secretes, in places of its choosing, with a shroud's light touch. Such was not this man whose walking the low-hanging veil of the lunar landscape appeared not to hinder. The raging frost brushed his forehead lightly without seeming *personal*. A road extending, a path diverging are consistent with the forward thrust of thought humming. In the winter night miraculously clean, because it was common to those dwelling in the universe who did not penetrate into it, the last player would no longer exist. He had lost every tie with the ancient swell of springs favorable to questioning, with the joyous bodies he had pleased to quicken near his own when he could still assign a summit to his pleasure, a snowfall to his talent. Today he broke off with sadness having become a hardened object, with the dread of the accepted. Earth had warped his belief, earth, with its somewhat limited pace, with its saffron-hued imagining, its attrition rifted with the acts of monsters. No one would have to forget him, for self-interest had never aided him, had never sketched him whole to the others' gaze. Across the whitewashed ceiling of his room, birds had passed, but their flash had melted into his sleep.

The veil of the lunar landscape, now lifted high, unfolds its aromatic colors above this personage of whom I speak. He comes forth lit by the cold and forever turns his back on the springtime that does not exist.

M.A.C.

109

Le requin et la m

Je vois enfin la mer \
tranche de son croissa. \
la grande volière sauv. \
ron.

Quand je dis: *j'ai lev.* \
maillé le cœur, ce n'est ɲ \
ce pèse-néant dont la ru \
ma persuasion. Mais rien \
jusqu'ici n'est témoin al \
sommeiller, ma jeunesse accourir. C'est de cela seul qu'il faut tirer richesse immédiate et opérante. Ainsi, il y a un jour de pur dans l'année, un jour qui creuse sa galerie merveilleuse dans l'écume de la mer, un jour qui monte aux yeux pour couronner midi. Hier la noblesse était déserte, le rameau était distant de ses bourgeons. Le requin et la mouette ne communiquaient pas.

O Vous, arc-en-ciel de ce rivage polisseur, approchez le navire de son espérance. Faites que toute fin supposée soit une neuve innocence, un fiévreux en-avant pour ceux qui trébuchent dans la matinale lourdeur.

Bef my eyes at last the sea in its triple harmony; the sea sc thing with its crescent the dynasty of absurd sufferings; great aviary of the wild; the sea credulous as a convolvulus.

When I say *I've rescinded the law, I've gone past morality, I've armored the heart,* I am not trying to justify myself before that void-meter, whose rumor extends its palm beyond my persuasion. But nothing that till now watched me living and acting is a witness hereabouts. My shoulder is free to sleep, my youth to come running. From that alone can be drawn immediate, operative wealth. Therefore there is one pure day in the year, one day that digs its marvelous tunnel within the foam of the sea, one day that climbs to the eyes to crown noon. Yesterday nobility was deserted, the branch was distant from its buds. The shark and the sea gull did not communicate.

O You, rainbow of this polishing shore, bring the ship close in to her hope. Make every supposed end be a new innocence, a feverish forward march for those stumbling in the morning heaviness.

J.G.

111

RECHERCHE DE

1955

The Shark a

ore

We have within us on our temperate slope a series of songs *which accompany us, wings connecting our relaxed breathing to our highest fevers. Pieces almost banal, mild in their coloring, recessed in their contour, whose fabric bears nevertheless a tiny wound. Anyone may set an origin and an end to this questionable* redness.

In a time when death, docile to fake sorcerers, sullies the noblest possibilities, we do not hesitate to set free *every instant at our disposal. Or better, let us turn to the ipomea, this bindweed which the ultimate night hour refines and half opens, but which noontime condemns to closure. It would be unthinkable that the quietude, on whose reverse side it welcomes us precariously, should not be that which we had desired, for our noonday repose.*

M.A.C.

Pyrénées

Montagnes des grands abusés,
Aux sommet de vos tours fiévreuses
Faiblit la dernière clarté.

Rien que le vide et l'avalanche,
La détresse et le regret!

Tous ces troubadours mal-aimés
Ont vu blanchir dans un été
Leur doux royaume pessimiste.

Ah! la neige est inexorable
Qui aime qu'on souffre à ses pieds,
Qui veut que l'on meure glacé,
Quand on a vécu dans les sables.

Pyrenees

Mountain range of the great deceived,
At the summit of your fevered
Turrets the last light grows faint.

Only abyss and avalanche,
Pain never done, known to be vain.

The troubadours of rejected love
Have all seen blanch, within one summer,
Their dear kingdom of hopelessness.

Ah, the snow is merciless—
Loves men to suffer at her feet,
Wants men to face a freezing fate
After lives lived in the sand wilderness.

J.G.

Qu'il vive!

Ce pays n'est qu'un vœu de l'esprit, un contre-sépulcre.

Dans mon pays, les tendres preuves du printemps et les oiseaux mal habillés sont préférés aux buts lointains.

La vérité attend l'aurore à côté d'une bougie. Le verre de fenêtre est négligé. Qu'importe à l'attentif.

Dans mon pays, on ne questionne pas un homme ému.

Il n'y a pas d'ombre maligne sur la barque chavirée.

Bonjour à peine, est inconnu dans mon pays.

On n'emprunte que ce qui peut se rendre augmenté.

Il y a des feuilles, beaucoup de feuilles sur les arbres de mon pays. Les branches sont libres de n'avoir pas de fruits.

On ne croit pas à la bonne foi du vainqueur.

Dans mon pays, on remercie.

This country is but a wish of the spirit, a counter-sepulchre.

In my country, tender proofs of spring and badly-dressed birds are preferred to far-off goals.

Truth waits for dawn beside a candle. Window-glass is neglected. To the watchful, what does it matter?

In my country, we don't question a man deeply moved.

There is no malignant shadow on the capsized boat.

A cool hello is unknown in my country.

We borrow only what can be returned increased.

There are leaves, many leaves, on the trees of my country. The branches are free to bear no fruits.

We don't believe in the good faith of the victor.

In my country, we say thank you.

M.A.C.

125

Grège

La Fête, c'est le ciel d'un bleu belliqueux et à la même seconde le temps au précipité orageux. C'est un risque dont le regard nous suit et nous maintient, soit qu'il nous interpelle, soit qu'il se ravise. C'est le grand emportement contre un ordre avantageux pour en faire jaillir un amour . . . Et sortir vainqueur de la Fête, c'est, lorsque cette main sur notre épaule nous murmure: «Pas si vite . . .», cette main dont l'équivoque s'efforce de retarder le retour à la mort, de se jeter dans l'irréalisable de la Fête.

L'amoureuse en secret

Elle a mis le couvert et mené à la perfection ce à quoi son amour assis en face d'elle parlera bas tout à l'heure, en la dévisageant. Cette nourriture semblable à l'anche d'un hautbois.

Sous la table, ses chevilles nues caressent à présent la chaleur du bien-aimé, tandis que des voix qu'elle n'entend pas, la complimentent. Le rayon de la lampe emmêle, tisse sa distraction sensuelle.

Un lit, très loin, sait-elle, patiente et tremble dans l'exil des draps odorants, comme un lac de montagne qui ne sera jamais abandonné.

Greige[8]

The Revels, a sky of bellicose blue, and in the same instant, a season of stormy precipitate. A risk whose gaze follows and maintains us, whether it challenges us or desists. The passion against an advantageous order so that a love may spring therefrom. And to exit victorious from the Revels, when this hand on our shoulder murmurs: "Not so fast. . . ,"—this hand whose ambivalence tries to delay the return to death—is to cast oneself into the unrealizable of the Revels.

M.A.C.

Loving in Secret

She has set the table and brought to perfection what her love seated across from her will speak to softly in a moment, looking hard at her. This food like the reed of an oboe.

Under the table, her bare ankles now caress the warmth of the one she loves, while voices she does not hear commend her. The lamp's beams tangle, weaving her sensual distraction.

She knows a bed, far off, awaits and trembles in the exile of sweet-smelling sheets, like a mountain lake never to be abandoned.

M.A.C.

[8] Greige: a color, a girl's name, and a distant reference to another civilization—"le feu grégeois" meaning fireworks, Greek fire.

127

Montagne déchirée

Oh! la toujours plus rase solitude
Des larmes qui montent aux cimes.

Quand se déclare la débâcle
Et qu'un vieil aigle sans pouvoir
Voit revenir son assurance,
Le bonheur s'élance à son tour,
A flanc d'abîme les rattrape.

Chasseur rival, tu n'as rien appris,
Toi qui sans hâte me dépasses
Dans la mort que je contredis.

Le Rébanqué, Lagnes, 29 août 1949.

Torn Mountain

Oh! ever barer solitude
Of the tears rising to the peaks.

When the collapse arrives
And an old eagle without power
Sees his confidence come back,
Happiness in its turn shoots forth,
Catching them at the verge of the abyss.

Rival hunter, you've learned nothing,
You who without haste move ahead
Into death that I contradict.

Le Rébanqué, Lagnes, August 29, 1949

J.G.

129

L'adolescent souffleté

Les mêmes coups qui l'envoyaient au sol le lançaient en même temps loin devant sa vie, vers les futures années où, quand il saignerait, ce ne serait plus à cause de l'iniquité d'un seul. Tel l'arbuste que réconfortent ses racines et qui presse ses rameaux meurtris contre son fût résistant, il descendait ensuite à reculons dans le mutisme de ce savoir et dans son innocence. Enfin il s'échappait, s'enfuyait et devenait souverainement heureux. Il atteignait la prairie et la barrière des roseaux dont il cajolait la vase et percevait le sec frémissement. Il semblait que ce que la terre avait produit de plus noble et de plus persévérant, l'avait, en compensation, adopté.

Il recommencerait ainsi jusqu'au moment où, la nécessité de rompre disparue, il se tiendrait droit et attentif parmi les hommes, à la fois plus vulnérable et plus fort.

The same blows that cast him to the ground projected him at once far ahead into his life, toward the future years when, wounded, he would no longer bleed from the iniquity of one being. Like the bush solaced by its roots, pressing its bruised boughs against its resistant bole, he would then descend backward into the silence of this knowledge and into its innocence. At last he escaped fleeing, and attained a sovereign happiness. He reached the meadow and the barrier of reeds whose slime he coaxed and whose dry quivering he watched. It seemed that the noblest and most enduring things that the earth had brought forth had, in compensation, adopted him.

Thus he would start again until, no longer needing to break off the battle, he could hold himself upright and attentive among men, more vulnerable and yet stronger.

M.A.C.

Recours au ruisseau

Sur l'aire du courant, dans les joncs agités, j'ai retracé ta ville. Les maçons au large feutre sont venus; ils se sont appliqués à suivre mon mouvement. Ils ne concevaient pas ma construction. Leur compétence s'alarmait.

Je leur ai dit que, confiante, tu attendais proche de là que j'eusse atteint la demie de ma journée pour connaître mon travail. A ce moment, notre satisfaction commune l'effacerait, nous le recommencerions plus haut, identiquement, dans la certitude de notre amour. Railleurs, ils se sont écartés. Je voyais, tandis qu'ils remettaient leur veste de toile, le gravier qui brillait dans le ciel du ruisseau et dont je n'avais, moi, nul besoin.

Le masque funèbre

Il était un homme, une fois, qui n'ayant plus faim, plus jamais faim, tant il avait dévoré d'héritages, englouti d'aliments, appauvri son prochain, trouva sa table vide, son lit désert, sa femme grosse, et la terre mauvaise dans le champ de son cœur.

N'ayant pas de tombeau et se voulant en vie, n'ayant rien à donner et moins à recevoir, les objets le fuyant, les bêtes lui mentant, il vola la famine et s'en fit une assiette qui devint son miroir et sa propre déroute.

132

Recourse to the Stream

On the surface of the current, among the quivering rushes, I retraced your town. The masons came with their broad felt hats; they endeavored to follow my movement. They could make no sense of my plan. Their competence took fright.

I told them that, in your confidence, you were awaiting nearby for me to finish half my day so as to know of my work. At that moment, our common satisfaction effacing it, we would begin it again unchanged, higher up, in the certainty of our love. Scoffing, they withdrew. I saw, as they donned once more their canvas jackets, the gravel sparkling in the sky of the stream, of which I, for my part, had no need.

M.A.C.

The Death Mask

There was a man, once, who being no longer ever hungry, what with all the legacies he had devoured, food he had guzzled, neighbours he had impoverished, found his table bare, his bed deserted, his wife pregnant, and the soil bad in the field of his heart.

Having no tomb and wanting to be alive, having nothing to give and less to receive, with objects shunning him, animals lying to him, he stole famine and made of it a dish that became his mirror and his own rout.

J.G.

Les lichens

Je marchais parmi les bosses d'une terre écurée, les haleines secrètes, les plantes sans mémoire. La montagne se levait, flacon empli d'ombre qu'étreignait par instant le geste de la soif. Ma trace, mon existence se perdaient. Ton visage glissait à reculons devant moi. Ce n'était qu'une tache à la recherche de l'abeille qui la ferait fleur et la dirait vivante. Nous allions nous séparer. Tu demeurerais sur le plateau des arômes et je pénétrerais dans le jardin du vide. Là, sous la sauvegarde des rochers, dans la plénitude du vent, je demanderais à la nuit véritable de disposer de mon sommeil pour accroître ton bonheur. Et tous les fruits t'appartiendraient.

The Lichens

I walked among the hummocks of a land scoured, the secret breaths, the plants without memory. The mountain rose up, a shadow-filled flask embraced now and again by the gesture of thirst. My track, my existence were slowly fading. Your face slipped away retreating in front of me. It was only a spot in search of the bee that would make of it a flower and call it alive. We were going to separate. You would remain on the high plain of scents and I would enter the garden of the void. There, in the safekeeping of rocks, in the wind's fullness, I would place my sleep at the disposition of the true night for it to deepen your happiness. And all the fruits would be yours by right.

M.A.C.

Joue et dors . . .

Joue et dors, bonne soif, nos oppresseurs ici ne sont pas
  sévères.
Volontiers ils plaisantent ou nous tiennent le bras
Pour traverser la périlleuse saison.
Sans doute, le poison s'est-il assoupi en eux,
Au point de desserrer leur barbare humeur.
Comme ils nous ont pourtant pourchassés jusqu'ici, ma
  soif,
Et contraints à vivre dans l'abandon de notre amour
  réduit à une mortelle providence!
Aromates, est-ce pour vous? Ou toutes plantes qui luttez
  sous un mur de sécheresse, est-ce pour vous? Ou nuages
  au grand large, prenant congé de la colonne?
Dans l'immense, comment deviner?

Qu'entreprendre pour fausser compagnie à ces tyrans,
  ô mon amie?
Joue et dors, que je mesure bien nos chances.
Mais, si tu me viens en aide, je devrais t'entraîner
  avec moi, et je ne veux pas t'exposer.
Alors, restons encore . . . Et qui pourrait nous dire lâches?

136

Play and Sleep . . .

Play and sleep, good thirst, our oppressors here are not
   being strict.
They like joking or holding our arm
To cross the dangerous season.
The poison must have dozed off in them,
Even unclenched their barbarian mood.
And yet how they have hunted us so far, my thirst,
And forced us to live in the abandon of our love,
   and it reduced to a mortal providence!
Aromatic herbs, is it for your sake? Or all you plants that
   struggle under a wall of dryness, is it for yours? Or you
   clouds in the open, taking leave of the column?
In the immensity, how guess?

What way is there of giving the slip to these tyrants,
   O my dearest?
Play and sleep, while I work out our chances.
But, if you come to my help, I would have to take you
   along with me, and I don't want to expose you.
So, let us stay longer . . . And who could call us
   cowards?

J.G.

137

Les inventeurs

Ils sont venus, les forestiers de l'autre versant, les inconnus
    de nous, les rebelles à nos usages.
Ils sont venus nombreux.
Leur troupe est apparue à la ligne de partage des cèdres
Et du champ de la vieille moisson désormais irrigué et vert.
La longue marche les avait échauffés.
Leur casquette cassait sur leurs yeux et leur pied fourbu
    se posait dans le vague.
Ils nous ont aperçus et se sont arrêtés.
Visiblement ils ne présumaient pas nous trouver là,
Sur des terres faciles et des sillons bien clos,
Tout à fait insouciants d'une audience.
Nous avons levé le front et les avons encouragés.

Le plus disert s'est approché, puis un second tout aussi
    déraciné et lent.
Nous sommes venus, dirent-ils, vous prévenir de l'arrivée
    prochaine de l'ouragan, de votre implacable adversaire.
Pas plus que vous, nous ne le connaissons
Autrement que par des relations et des confidences
    d'ancêtres.
Mais pourquoi sommes-nous heureux incompréhensible-
    ment devant vous et soudain pareils à des enfants?

Nous avons dit merci et les avons congédiés.
Mais auparavant ils ont bu, et leurs mains tremblaient,
    et leurs yeux riaient sur les bords.
Hommes d'arbres et de cognée, capables de tenir tête à
    quelque terreur, mais inaptes à conduire l'eau, à aligner
    des bâtisses, à les enduire de couleurs plaisantes,
Ils ignoreraient le jardin d'hiver et l'économie de la joie.

138

The Inventors

They came, the foresters of the other slope, men unknown
to us, resistant to our customs.
They came in numbers.
Their party appeared at the dividing line between the
cedars
And the field of the old harvest henceforth watered and
green.
The long walk had heated them.
Their caps were crushed over their eyes and their tired-out
feet trod in the uncertain.
They caught sight of us and stopped.
Evidently they did not expect to find us there,
On easy lands and furrows tightly closed,
Completely unconcerned about an audience.
We looked up and encouraged them.

The most eloquent stepped nearer, then a second one no
less uprooted and slow.
We have come, they said, to warn you of the imminent
arrival of the hurricane, of your implacable adversary.
No more than you do we know of it
Except by ancestors' tales and secrets.
But why are we incomprehensibly happy before you and
suddenly like children?

We said our thanks and bade them leave.
But first they drank, and their hands trembled, and their
eyes laughed at the edges.
Men of trees and of axes able to face any terror, but
unskilled at conveying water, at aligning houses, at
plastering them in pleasing colors,
Of the garden of winter they knew nothing nor of the
economy of joy.

Certes, nous aurions pu les convaincre et les conquérir,
Car l'angoisse de l'ouragan est émouvante.
Oui, l'ouragan allait bientôt venir;
Mais cela valait-il la peine que l'on en parlât et qu'on
    dérangeât l'avenir?
Là où nous sommes, il n'y a pas de crainte urgente.

Sivergues, 30 septembre 1949.

Certainly, we could have convinced them and conquered
  them.
For the anguish of the hurricane is moving.
Yes, the hurricane was soon to come;
But was it worth mentioning and disquieting the future?
Where we are, there's no pressing fear.

Sivergues, September 30, 1949

M.A.C.

LA PAROLE EN ARCHIPEL

1952-1960

THE WORD AS ARCHIPELAGO

1952-1960

LA PAROI ET LA PRAIRIE

Lascaux

I. *Homme-oiseau mort et bison mourant*

Long corps qui eut l'enthousiasme exigeant,
A présent perpendiculaire à la Brute blessée.

O tué sans entrailles!
Tué par celle qui fut tout et, réconciliée, se meurt;
Lui, danseur d'abîme, esprit, toujours à naître,
Oiseau et fruit pervers des magies cruellement sauvé.

II. *Les cerfs noirs*

Les eaux parlaient à l'oreille du ciel.
Cerfs, vous avez franchi l'espace millénaire,
Des ténèbres du roc aux caresses de l'air.

Le chasseur qui vous pousse, le génie qui vous voit,
Que j'aime leur passion, de mon large rivage!
Et si j'avais leurs yeux, dans l'instant où j'espère?

III. *La Bête innommable*

La Bête innommable ferme la marche du gracieux
    troupeau, comme un cyclope bouffe.
Huit quolibets font sa parure, divisent sa folie.
La Bête rote dévotement dans l'air rustique.
Ses flancs bourrés et tombants sont douloureux,
    vont se vider de leur grossesse.
De son sabot à ses vaines défenses, elle est enveloppée
    de fétidité.

Ainsi m'apparaît dans la frise de Lascaux, mère
    fantastiquement déguisée,
La Sagesse aux yeux pleins de larmes.

144

THE ROCK-WALL AND THE MEADOW
(complete text)

Lascaux

I. *Dead Bird-man and Dying Bison*

Thin body that had imperious enthusiasm,
Now perpendicular to the wounded Brute.

O killed without any pity!
Killed by what was all and, reconciled, is dying;
He, the abyss dancer, spirit, yet to be born,
Bird and perverse fruit of magics, cruelly saved.

II. *The Black Stag*

The waters spoke on into the sky's ear.
Stag, you and you and you have crossed millennia, the
     space
From rock darkness to the air's caresses.

The hunter driving you, the genius seeking you—
How, from my broad shore, I love their passions!
And if their eyes were mine, at the instant when I hope?

III. *The Beast Not To Be Named*

The beast not to be named closes the march of the dainty
     herd, like a comic cyclops.
Eight jibes make up her finery, share out her folly.
The beast belches a prayer into the country air.
Her stuffed and sagging flanks are hurting, will
     soon rid themselves of their bigness.
From her hooves to her vain tusks she is muffled in stench.

This is how, in the Lascaux frieze, to me appears,
     mother in fantastical disguise,
Wisdom with her eyes full of tears.

IV. *Jeune cheval à la crinière vaporeuse*

Que tu es beau, printemps, cheval,
Criblant le ciel de ta crinière,
Couvrant d'écume les roseaux!
Tout l'amour tient dans ton poitrail:
De la Dame blanche d'Afrique
A la Madeleine au miroir,
L'idole qui combat, la grâce qui médite.

IV. *Colt with Mane of Spray*

You are a beauty, springtime, colt,
As you splash the sky with your mane
And cover the bulrushes with foam!
The whole of love dwells in your chest:
From the pale-face Lady of Africa
To the Magdalen with the mirror,
Idol that fights, and grace that meditates.

Cette part jamais fixée, en nous sommeillante,
d'où jaillira DEMAIN LE MULTIPLE.

L'âge du renne, c'est-à-dire l'âge du souffle.
O vitre, ô givre, nature conquise, dedans fleurie,
dehors détruite!

Insouciants, nous exaltons et contrecarrons justement
la nature et les hommes. Cependant, terreur, au-dessus
de notre tête, le soleil entre dans le signe de ses
ennemis.

La lutte contre la cruauté profane, hélas, voeu de fourmi
ailée. Sera-t-elle notre novation?

Au soleil d'hiver quelques fagots noués et ma flamme au
mur.

Terre où je m'endors, espace où je m'éveille, qui viendra
quand vous ne serez plus là? (*que deviendrai-je* m'est
d'une chaleur presque infinie).

Chilling

This never stilled part, slumbering in us, from which
will spring TOMORROW THE MANIFOLD.

The age of the reindeer,—that is, the age of breathing.
O window-pane, O hoarfrost, nature conquered, in
flower within, outside destroyed!

Thoughtlessly we exalt and oppose nature and men,
nothing less. Meanwhile, terror overhead,
the sun is entering the sign of his enemies.

The struggle against profane cruelty, alas, a winged
ant's vow. Will it be our renewal?

In the winter sunshine a few bundles of fagots and
my fire by the wall.

Earth on which I go to sleep, space into which I wake,
who will come when you are no longer there?
(*what shall I become* has for me an almost infinite
warmth).

Quatre fascinants

I. *Le taureau*

Il ne fait jamais nuit quand tu meurs,
Cerné de ténèbres qui crient,
Soleil aux deux pointes semblables.

Fauve d'amour, vérité dans l'épée,
Couple qui se poignarde unique parmi tous.

II. *La truite*

Rives qui croulez en parure
Afin d'emplir tout le miroir,
Gravier où balbutie la barque
Que le courant presse et retrousse,
Herbe, herbe toujours étirée,
Herbe, herbe jamais en répit,
Que devient votre créature
Dans les orages transparents
Où son cœur la précipita?

III. *Le serpent*

Prince des contresens, fais que mon amour
En exil analogue à ton bannissement
Echappe au vieux Seigneur que je hais d'avoir pu,
Après l'avoir troublé, en clair le décevoir.

Revanche à tes couleurs, débonnaire serpent,
Sous le couvert du bois et en toute maison.
Par le lien qui unit la lumière à la peur,
Tu fais semblant de fuir, ô serpent marginal!

150

Four Ensorcelers

I. *The Bull*

It is never night when you die
Ringed about with shadows that cry,
Sun with the two matched points.

Love's wild beast, truth in the sword;
Nonpareil couple stabbing each other.

II. *The Trout*

Banks crumbling in finery
To fill the entire mirror full,
Gravel against which the boat stutters
As the stream pushes it and pulls,
Grass, grass always stretched,
Grass, grass never let rest,
What becomes of this your creature
In the transparent storms to which
Its heart pitched it?

III. *The Serpent*

Prince of anti-order, make my love
In some exile like your banishment
Escape the old Lord I hate because he could
Stir it first, then openly disappoint.

Vengeance for your colors, debonair serpent,
Under the wood's cover and in each house.
By that bond which joins fear and light
You feign flight, O margin-haunting serpent.

IV. *L'alouette*

Extrême braise du ciel et première ardeur du jour,
Elle reste sertie dans l'aurore et chante la terre agitée,
Carillon maître de son haleine et libre de sa route.

Fascinante, on la tue en l'émerveillant.

IV. *The Lark*

Remotest glow of the sky and first fire of day,
She remains set in dawn, and sings of the restless earth,
Peal of bells, in control of her breath and free to choose
  her way.

She who ensorcels can be dazzled down to death.

La Minutieuse

L'inondation s'agrandissait. La campagne rase, les talus, les menus arbres désunis s'enfermaient dans des flaques dont quelques-unes en se joignant devenaient lac. Une alouette au ciel trop gris chantait. Des bulles çà et là brisaient la surface des eaux à moins que ce ne fut quelque minuscule rongeur ou serpent s'échappant à la nage. La route encore restait intacte. Les abords d'un village se montraient. Résolus et heureux nous avancions. Dans notre errance il faisait beau. Je marchais entre Toi et cette Autre qui était Toi. Dans chacune de mes mains je tenais serré votre sein nu. Des villageois sur le pas de leur porte ou occupés à quelque besogne de planche nous saluaient avec faveur. Mes doigts leur cachaient votre merveille. En eussent-ils été choqués? L'une de vous s'arrêta pour causer et pour sourire. Nous continuâmes. J'avais désormais la nature à ma droite et devant moi la route. Un boeuf au loin, en son milieu, nous précédait. La lyre de ses cornes, il me parut, tremblait. Je t'aimais. Mais je reprochais à celle qui était demeurée en chemin, parmi les habitants des maisons, de se montrer trop familière. Certes, elle ne pouvait figurer parmi nous que ton enfance attardée. Je me rendis à l'évidence. Au village la retiendraient l'école et cette façon qu'ont les communautés aguerries de temporiser avec le danger. Même celui de l'inondation. Maintenant, nous avions atteint l'orée de très vieux arbres et la solitude des souvenirs. Je voulus m'enquérir de ton nom éternel et chéri que mon âme avait oublié: "Je suis la Minutieuse." La beauté des eaux profondes nous endormit.

Thoroughgo

The flood was rising. The level meadows, knolls and small isolated trees were being shut away in pools, some of which, joining, became a lake. In the too grey sky there was a lark, singing. Here and there bubbles broke the waters' surface, unless it was some tiny rodent or snake escaping by swimming. Our road was still untouched. The outskirts of a village came into sight. Resolute and happy, we went forward. In our wandering the day was fine. I was walking between You and that Other who also was You. In each of my hands I held close your naked breast. Villagers on their doorsteps or busy at some plankwork greeted us in a friendly way. My fingers hid your miracle from them. Would it have shocked them? One of you stopped to chat and smile. We went on. Now I had country on my right and in front the road. In the middle of it an ox preceded us, a good way ahead. The lyre of its horns was, I thought, trembling. I was in love with you. But I kept reproaching the one who had stopped by the wayside, among the inhabitants of the houses, for showing herself too familiar. Of course, among us, she could only represent your lingering childhood. I saw this clearly. What would be keeping her in the village was the school, and the way seasoned communities have of temporising with a danger. Even of flood. We had come now to the edge of some very old trees and the solitude of memories. I wanted to ask your eternal and cherished name, which my soul had forgotten: "I am Thoroughgo." The beauty of the deep waters gathered us to slumber.

J.G.

L'inoffensif

Je pleure quand le soleil se couche parce qu'il te dérobe à ma vue et parce que je ne sais pas m'accorder avec ses rivaux nocturnes. Bien qu'il soit au bas et maintenant sans fièvre, impossible d'aller contre son déclin, de suspendre son effeuillaison, d'arracher quelque envie encore à sa lueur moribonde. Son départ te fond dans son obscurité comme le limon du lit se délaye dans l'eau du torrent par delà l'éboulis des berges détruites. Dureté et mollesse au ressort différent ont alors des effets semblables. Je cesse de recevoir l'hymne de ta parole; soudain tu n'apparais plus entière à mon côté; ce n'est pas le fuseau nerveux de ton poignet que tient ma main mais la branche creuse d'un quelconque arbre mort et déjà débité. On ne met plus un nom à rien, qu'au frisson. Il fait nuit. Les artifices qui s'allument me trouvent aveugle.

Je n'ai pleuré en vérité qu'une seule fois. Le soleil en disparaissant avait coupé ton visage. Ta tête avait roulé dans la fosse du ciel et je ne croyais plus au lendemain.

Lequel est l'homme du matin et lequel celui des ténèbres?

156

I weep when the sun sets, because he screens you from my sight and because I never can come to terms with his nocturnal rivals. Although he is low and now without fever, impossible to go against his decline, to suspend his unleafing, to wrench some desire still from his moribund glow. His departure melts you into his dark as the silt from the torrent's bed merges into the water below where the banks have crumbled. Hard and soft with differing mainsprings then have like effects. I cease receiving the hymn of your speech; suddenly you appear no longer whole, there at my side; what my hand is holding is no longer the nervy spindle of your wrist, but a hollow branch from some dead, already chopped tree. One can't now put a name to anything, except the shudder. It is night. The kindling lures find me blind.

I wept only once, really. The sun in vanishing had cut off your face. Your head had rolled into the pit of the sky and I no longer believed in tomorrow.

Which is the man of the morning and which the one of the dark?

J.G.

Le mortel partenaire

A Maurice Blanchot.

Il la défiait, s'avançait vers son cœur, comme un boxeur ourlé, ailé et puissant, bien au centre de la géométrie attaquante et défensive de ses jambes. Il pesait du regard les qualités de l'adversaire qui se contentait de rompre, cantonné entre une virginité agréable et son expérience. Sur la blanche surface où se tenait le combat, tous deux oubliaient les spectateurs inexorables. Dans l'air de juin voltigeait le prénom des fleurs du premier jour de l'été. Enfin une légère grimace courut sur la joue du second et une raie rose s'y dessina. La riposte jaillit sèche et conséquente. Les jarrets soudain comme du linge étendu, l'homme flotta et tituba. Mais les poings en face ne poursuivirent pas leur avantage, renoncèrent à conclure. A présent les têtes meurtries des deux battants dodelinaient l'une contre l'autre. A cet instant le premier dut à dessein prononcer à l'oreille du second des paroles si parfaitement offensantes, ou appropriées, ou énigmatiques, que de celui-ci fila, prompte, totale, précise, une foudre qui coucha net l'incompréhensible combattant.

Certains êtres ont une signification qui nous manque. Qui sont-ils? Leur secret tient au plus profond du secret même de la vie. Ils s'en approchent. Elle les tue. Mais l'avenir qu'ils ont ainsi éveillé d'un murmure, les devinant, les crée. O dédale de l'extrême amour!

158

The Mortal Partner

He challenged it, advanced toward its heart, like a hemmed, winged, and powerful boxer, exactly in the center of the attacking and defending geometry of his legs. His look surmised the capabilities of his adversary who was satisfied to give up the battle, midway between an agreeable virginity and his experience. On the white surface where the combat was taking place, both forgot the inexorable spectators. In the June air the given name of the flowers on the summer's first day spun about. Finally a slight grimace ran over the cheek of the adversary and a rosy streak was sketched there. The riposte spurted out brusque and consistent. His legs suddenly like linen stretched, the man tossed and swayed. But the facing fists did not follow through on their advantage, abandoned the wind-up. Now the bruised heads of the two combatants bobbed against each other. At that moment the first opponent must have purposely pronounced in the second's ear such offensive or appropriate or enigmatic words that from the latter there came instantly, total and precise, a bolt of lightning which laid low the incomprehensible attacker.

Certain beings have a meaning that escapes us. Who are they? Their secret resides in the depths of the very secret of life. They approach it. It kills them. But the future which they have thus awakened with a murmur, finding them out, creates them. Oh labyrinth of extreme love!

M.A.C.

Front de la rose

Malgré la fenêtre ouverte dans la chambre au long congé, l'arôme de la rose reste lié au souffle qui fut là. Nous sommes une fois encore sans expérience antérieure, nouveaux venus, épris. La rose! Le champ de ses allées éventerait même la hardiesse de la mort. Nulle grille qui s'oppose. Le désir resurgit, mal de nos fronts évaporés.

Celui qui marche sur la terre des pluies n'a rien à redouter de l'épine, dans les lieux finis ou hostiles. Mais s'il s'arrête et se recueille, malheur à lui! Blessé au vif, il vole en cendres, archer repris par la beauté.

Brow of the Rose

Despite the window open in the room of long leave, the rose fragrance remains joined to the breath which was there. Once again we are without prior experience, newcomers, in love. The rose! The field of its moving paths would fan away even death's boldness. No gate to make opposition. Desire surges up afresh, disorder of our flighty foreheads.

He who walks on the earth of rains has nothing to fear from the thorn, in places finite or hostile. But should he stop to meditate, woe to him! Wounded to the quick, he flies to ashes, archer recaptured by beauty.

M.A.C.

Marmonnement

Pour ne pas me rendre et pour m'y retrouver, je t'offense, mais combien je suis épris de toi, loup, qu'on dit à tort funèbre, pétri des secrets de mon arrière-pays. C'est dans une masse d'amour légendaire que tu laisses la déchaussure vierge, pourchassée de ton ongle. Loup, je t'appelle, mais tu n'as pas de réalité nommable. De plus, tu es inintelligible. Non-comparant, compensateur, que sais-je? Derrière ta course sans crinière, je saigne, je pleure, je m'enserre de terreur, j'oublie, je ris sous les arbres. Traque impitoyable où l'on s'acharne, où tout est mis en action contre la double proie: toi invisible et moi vivace.

Continue, va, nous durons ensemble; et ensemble, bien que séparés, nous bondissons par-dessus le frisson de la suprême déception pour briser la glace des eaux vives et se reconnaître là.

Mumbling

Not to surrender and so to take my bearings, I offend you, but how in love with you I am, wolf, wrongly called funereal, moulded with the secrets of my back country. In a mass of legendary love you leave the trace, virgin, hunted, of your claw.[9] Wolf, I call you, but you have no nameable reality. Moreover, you are unintelligible. By default, compensating, what else could I say? Behind your maneless running, I am bleeding, weeping; I gird myself with terror, I forget, I am laughing under the trees. Pitiless and unending pursuit, where all is set in motion against the double prey: you invisible and I perennial.

Go on, we endure together; and together, although separate, we bound over the tremor of supreme deception to shatter the ice of quick waters and recognize ourselves there.

M.A.C.

[9] This should be read as if a comma had been placed after the word "pourchassée."

Marmonnement

Pour ne pas me rendre et pour m'y retrouver
je t'offense, mais combien je suis épris de
toi, loup, qu'on dit à tort funèbre, pétri
des secrets de mon arrière-pays. C'est dans
une masse d'amour légendaire que tu laisses
la déchaussure vierge, pourchassé de ton
ongle. Loup, je t'appelle, mais tu n'as
pas de réalité nommable. De plus, tu
es inintelligible. Non-comparant, com-
pensateur, que sais-je? Derrière ta course
sans crinière ~~visage~~, je saigne, je pleure, je m'ensemence
de terreur, j'oublie, je ris sous les arbres.
Traque impitoyable où l'on s'acharne,
où tout est mis en action contre la
double proie: toi invisible et moi vivace.
    Continue, va, nous durons ensemble;
et ensemble, bien que séparés, ~~nous~~
~~brisons la glace des ~~tremaux~~~~, nous bon-
dissons par-dessus le frisson de la
suprême déception ~~pour briser la glace~~ ~~mais que d'autres~~
~~des eaux vives et ~~mettre en pièces qui ores vivaces~~~~
~~que nous? et reconnaître le soleil pour les~~
~~forces bienfaisantes qui, grâce à ses~~

(31 janvier 1954)
René Char

Original manuscript of the poem "Marmonnement" from *Le Nu perdu*, 1972. Private collection of the poet. (Previously un-published)

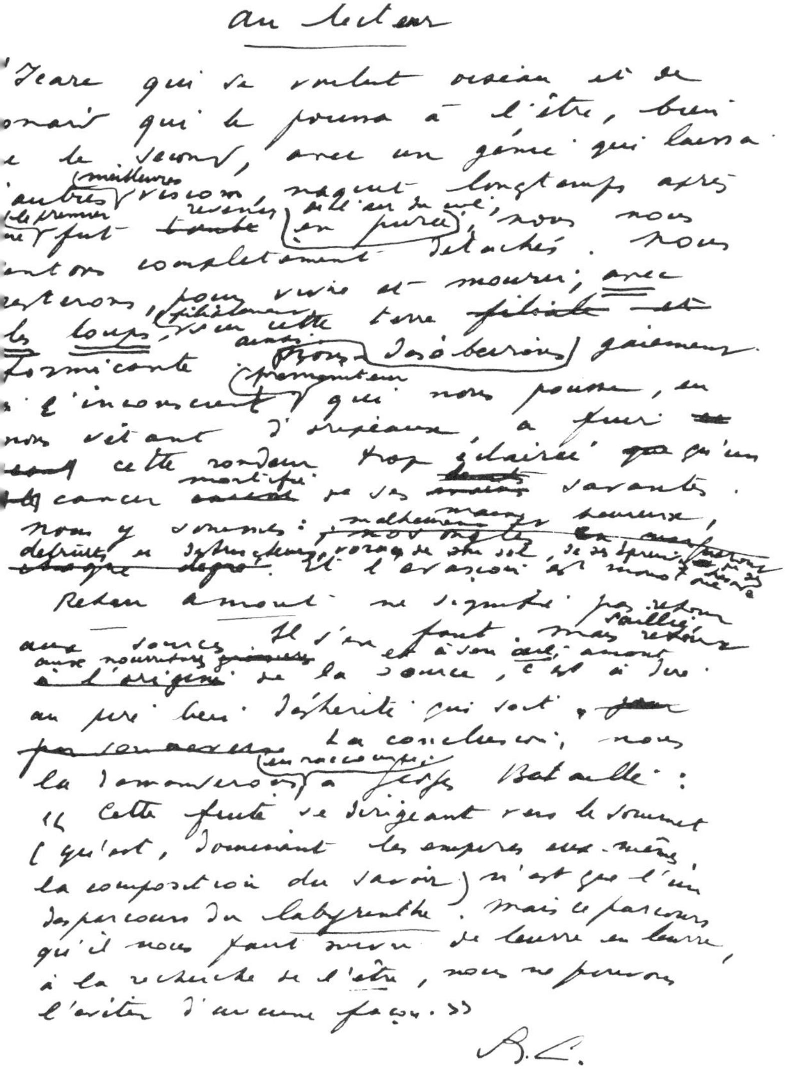

au lecteur

[Handwritten manuscript text, largely illegible]

R.C.

Original manuscript of the text "Au Lecteur," in *Retour amont*, 1966. Private collection of the poet. (Previously unpublished)

Le risque et le pendule

A René Ménard.

Toi qui ameutes et qui passes entre l'épanouie et le voltigeur, sois celui pour qui le papillon touche les fleurs du chemin.

Reste avec la vague à la seconde où son cœur expire. Tu verras.

Sensible aussi à la salive du rameau.

Sans plus choisir entre oublier et bien apprendre.

Puisses-tu garder au vent de ta branche tes amis essentiels.

Elle transporte le verbe, l'abeille frontalière qui, à travers haines ou embuscades, va pondre son miel sur la passade d'un nuage.

La nuit ne s'étonne plus du volet que l'homme tire.

Une poussière qui tombe sur la main occupée à tracer le poème, les foudroie, poème et main.

164

The Risk and the Clock

To René Ménard.

You who rouse and pass between the girl in bloom and the man on the trapeze, be the one for whom the butterfly touches the roadside flowers.

Stay with the wave at the second when its heart expires. You will see.

Sensible also of the bough's saliva.

No longer choosing between forgetting and really learning.

May you keep in the wind of your branch your essential friends.

She transports the word, does the borderer bee who, across hates or ambushes, goes to lay her honey on a cloud's fancy.

Night is no longer surprised at the shutter a man closes.

A speck of dust, that falls on the hand busy writing out the poem, blasts them, poem and hand.

J.G.

Nous nous sommes soudain trop approchés de quelque chose dont on nous tenait à une distance mystérieusement favorable et mesurée. Depuis lors, c'est le rongement. Notre appuie-tête a disparu.

Il est insupportable de se sentir part solidaire et impuissante d'une beauté en train de mourir par la faute d'autrui. Solidaire dans sa poitrine et impuissant dans le mouvement de son esprit.

Si ce que je te montre et ce que je te donne te semblent moindres que ce que je te cache, ma balance est pauvre, ma glane est sans vertu.

Tu es reposoir d'obscurité sur ma face trop offerte, poème. Ma splendeur et ma souffrance se sont glissées entre les deux.

Jeter bas l'existence laidement accumulée et retrouver le regard qui l'aima assez à son début pour en étaler le fondement. Ce qui me reste à vivre est dans cet assaut, dans ce frisson.

166

To Resume

Suddenly we drew too near to something from which we'd been held at a mysteriously favored and measured distance. Ever since, corrosion. Our head-rest has vanished.

It is unbearable to feel oneself a committed and impotent part of a beauty dying by the fault of another. Committed in one's breast and impotent in the movement of one's mind.

If what I show and what I give seem less to you than what I hide, my balance is poor, my reaping, without virtue.

You are, poem, the repository of darkness on my too exposed face. Between them my splendor and my suffering have found their narrow way.

To cast off existence, its ugly accumulation, and find again the gaze fond enough in its beginnings to bare its foundation. What I have left to live exists in this assault, in this tremor.

M.A.C.

Le bois de l'Epte

Je n'étais ce jour-là que deux jambes qui marchent.
Aussi, le regard sec, le nul au centre du visage,
Je me mis à suivre le ruisseau du vallon.
Bas coureur, ce fade ermite ne s'immisçait pas
Dans l'informe où je m'étendais toujours plus avant.

Venus du mur d'angle d'une ruine laissée jadis par
    l'incendie,
Plongèrent soudain dans l'eau grise
Deux rosiers sauvages pleins d'une douce et inflexible
    volonté.
Il s'y devinait comme un commerce d'êtres disparus, à
    la veille de s'annoncer encore.

Le rauque incarnat d'une rose, en frappant l'eau,
Rétablit la face première du ciel avec l'ivresse des
    questions,
Eveilla au milieu des paroles amoureuses la terre,
Ma poussa dans l'avenir comme un outil affamé et
    fiévreux.

Le bois de l'Epte commençait un tournant plus loin.
Mais je n'eus pas à le traverser, le cher grainetier du
    relèvement!
Je humai, sur le talon du demi-tour, le remugle des
    prairies où fondait une bête,
J'entendis glisser la peureuse couleuvre;
De chacun—ne me traitez pas durement—j'accomplissais,
    je le sus, les souhaits.

Epte Wood

That day I was merely two legs walking.
With dry gaze, the nought in the centre of my face,
I set out to follow the valley brook.
That drab hermit, crouched runner, did not intrude upon
The formlessness in which I kept extending on and on.

Sprung from a corner of ruined wall left long ago by a fire,
There plunged suddenly into the grey water
Two rose-shoots full of a sweet inflexible will.
In them one divined some commerce of vanished beings,
    on the eve of appearing once more.

The raucous incarnadine of a rose, striking the water,
Restored the primal face of the sky with the ecstasy of
    questions,
Awoke in a welter of loving words the earth,
Pushed me into the future like some famished and feverish
    implement.

Epte Wood began, one bend farther on,
But I'd no need to go through it, that dear seed-bed of the
    fresh start!
I breathed, on the heel of my about-turn, the reek of
    the meadows, into which an animal seemed just
    dissolving.
I heard the timid grass snake sliding;
Of every being—don't judge me harshly—I was, I knew,
    fulfilling the wishes.

J.G.

Victoire éclair

L'oiseau bêche la terre,
Le serpent sème,
La mort améliorée
Applaudit la récolte.

Pluton dans le ciel!

L'explosion en nous.
Là seulement dans moi.
Fol et sourd comment pourrais-je l'être davantage?

Plus de second soi-même, de visage changeant,
    plus de saison pour la flamme et de saison pour l'ombre!

Avec la lente neige descendent les lépreux.

Soudain l'amour, l'égal de la terreur,
D'une main jamais vue arrête l'incendie, redresse le
    soleil, reconstruit l'Amie.

Rien n'annonçait une existence si forte.

Lightning Victory

The bird hoes the ground,
The serpent sows,
Death the gainer
Applauds the harvest.

Pluto in the sky!

Explosion in us.
There in myself only.
Mad and deaf, how could I be more so?

No more second self, or changing face, no more
   a season for flame and a season for shadow!

With the slow snow descend the lepers.

Suddenly love, terror's equal,
With hand never seen checks the fire,
   restores the sun, reconstructs the Beloved.

Nothing gave notice of a life so strong.

J.G.

La chambre dans l'espace

Tel le chant du ramier quand l'averse est prochaine—l'air se poudre de pluie, de soleil revenant—, je m'éveille lavé, je fonds en m'élevant; je vendange le ciel novice.

Allongé contre toi, je meus ta liberté. Je suis un bloc de terre qui réclame sa fleur.

Est-il gorge menuisée plus radieuse que la tienne? Demander c'est mourir!

L'aile de ton soupir met un duvet aux feuilles. Le trait de mon amour ferme ton fruit, le boit.

Je suis dans la grâce de ton visage que mes ténèbres couvrent de joie.

Comme il est beau ton cri qui me donne ton silence!

172

The Room in Space

Like the wood-pigeon's song when the shower is near—
the air is powdered with rain, with haunting sunshine—,
I awake washed, I melt in rising; I vintage the newcomer
sky.

Lying beside you, I move your liberty. I am a clod of
earth claiming its flower.

Is there a finely worked throat more radiant than yours?
To ask is to die!

The wing of your sigh makes the leaves downy.
The shaft of my love closes your fruit, drinks it.

I am here in the grace of your face, which my darknesses
cover with joy.

How beautiful your cry that gives me your silence!

J.G.

Rapport de marée

Terre et ciel ont-ils renoncé à leurs féeries saisonnières, à leurs palabres subtiles? Se sont-ils soumis? Pas plus celle-ci que celui-là n'ont encore, il semble, de projets pour eux, de bonheur pour nous.

Une branche s'éveille aux paroles dorées de la lampe, une branche dans une eau fade, un rameau sans avenir. Le regard s'en saisit, voyage. Puis, de nouveau, tout languit, patiente, se balance et souffre. L'acanthe simule la mort. Mais, cette fois, nous ne ferons pas route ensemble.

Bien-aimée, derrière ma porte?

Invitation

J'appelle les amours qui roués et suivis par la faulx de l'été, au soir embaument l'air de leur blanche inaction.

Il n'y a plus de cauchemar, douce insomnie perpétuelle. Il n'y a plus d'aversion. Que la pause d'un bal dont l'entrée est partout dans les nuées du ciel.

Je viens avant la rumeur des fontaines, au final du tailleur de pierre.

Sur ma lyre mille ans pèsent moins qu'un mort.

J'appelle les amants.

174

Tide Report

Have earth and sky abandoned their seasonal wonders, their subtle parley? Have they given in? No more the one than the other seems yet to have projects of its own, to hold any gladness for us.

A branch awakes to the lamp's gilded words, a branch in a pallid water, a bough without future. The gaze seizes it, journeys. Then, again, all languishes, waits, sways and suffers. The acanthus simulates death. But this time, we shall not travel together.

Beloved, behind my door?

M.A.C.

Invitation

I summon the loves that, racked and followed by summer's scythe, embalm the evening air with their white inactivity.

No longer nightmare, soft perpetual sleeplessness. No more aversion. Only the pause in a dance whose entrance is everywhere among the sky-drifts.

I come before the murmur of fountains, at the stone-cutter's finale.

On my lyre a thousand years weigh less than a dead man.

I summon the lovers.

M.A.C.

175

La bibliothèque est en feu

A Georges Braque.

Par la bouche de ce canon il neige. C'était l'enfer dans notre tête. Au même moment c'est le printemps au bout de nos doigts. C'est la foulée de nouveau permise, la terre en amour, les herbes exubérantes.

L'esprit aussi, comme toute chose, a tremblé.

L'aigle est au futur.

Toute action qui engage l'âme, quand bien même celle-ci en serait ignorante, aura pour épilogue un repentir ou un chagrin. Il faut y consentir.

Comment me vint l'écriture? Comme un duvet d'oiseau sur ma vitre, en hiver. Aussitôt s'éleva dans l'âtre une bataille de tisons qui n'a pas, encore à présent, pris fin.

Soyeuses villes du regard quotidien, insérées parmi d'autres villes, aux rues tracées par nous seuls, sous l'aile d'éclairs qui répondent à nos attentions.

Tout en nous ne devrait être qu'une fête joyeuse quand quelque chose que nous n'avons pas prévu, que nous n'éclairons pas, qui va parler à notre cœur, par ses seuls moyens, s'accomplit.

Continuons à jeter nos coups de sonde, à parler à voix égale, par mots groupés, nous finirons par faire taire tous ces chiens, par obtenir qu'ils se confondent avec l'herbage, nous surveillant d'un œil fumeux, tandis que le vent effacera leur dos.

L'éclair me dure.

Il n'y a que mon semblable, la compagne ou le compagnon, qui puisse m'éveiller de ma torpeur, déclencher

176

The Library Is on Fire

To Georges Braque.

From this cannon's mouth it is snowing. Hell was there in our head. At the same moment it's spring at our finger-tips. To stride again permitted, the earth in love, grasses overflowing.

The spirit too, like everything else, has quaked.

The eagle is in the future.

Every action that commits the soul, even though una-wares, will have as its epilogue a repenting or a sorrow. One has to consent to that.

How did writing come to me? Like bird's down on my window-pane, in winter. At once there arose in the fire-place a battle of embers which has not, even now, come to an end.

Silky cities of the daily look, inserted among other cities, with streets mapped out by us alone, under the wing of lightnings that respond to our solicitude.

Everything in us should be purely a joyful feast, when something that we did not foresee, that we do not light, that will speak to our heart, simply by its own means, is fulfilled.

Let us continue to take our soundings, to speak with an even voice, in grouped words, we shall end by silencing all these dogs, by getting them to melt into the grass, where they will watch us with a smoky eye while the wind rubs out their back.

Lightning lasts me.

Only my fellow human being, woman or man friend, can wake me from my torpor, let loose poetry, hurl me

la poésie, me lancer contre les limites du vieux désert afin que j'en triomphe. Aucun autre. Ni cieux, ni terre privilégiée, ni choses dont on tressaille.
Torche, je ne valse qu'avec lui.

On ne peut pas commencer un poème sans une parcelle d'erreur sur soi et sur le monde, sans une paille d'innocence aux premiers mots.

Dans le poème, chaque mot ou presque doit être employé dans son sens originel. Certains, se détachant, deviennent plurivalents. Il en est d'amnésiques. La constellation du Solitaire est tendue.

La poésie me volera ma mort.

Pourquoi *poème pulvérisé*? Parce qu'au terme de son voyage vers le Pays, après l'obscurité pré-natale et la dureté terrestre, la finitude du poème est lumière, apport de l'être à la vie.

Le poète ne retient pas ce qu'il découvre; l'ayant transcrit, le perd bientôt. En cela réside sa nouveauté, son infini et son péril.

Mon métier est un métier de pointe.

On naît avec les hommes, on meurt inconsolé parmi les dieux.

La terre qui reçoit la graine est triste. La graine qui va tant risquer est heureuse.

Il est une malédiction qui ne ressemble à aucune autre. Elle papillote dans une sorte de paresse, a une nature avenante, se compose un visage aux traits rassurants. Mais quel ressort, passée la feinte, quelle course immédiate au but! Probablement, car l'ombre où elle échafaude est maligne, la région parfaitement secrète, elle se soustraira à une appellation, s'esquivera toujours à temps. Elle

178

against the limits of the old desert, for me to triumph over it. No-one else. Not skies, nor favored country, nor things that set one quivering.

Torch, I waltz with him only.

One can't begin a poem without some scrap of error about oneself and the world, without some straw of innocence at the first words.

In the poem every word, or nearly, must be used in its original meaning. Some detach themselves and become plurivalent. There are amnesic ones. The constellation of the Solitary is taut.

Poetry will rob me of my death.

Why *pulverized poem*? Because at the term of its voyage toward the land, after the prenatal darkness and the terrestrial hardness, the end of the poem is light, a being's contribution to life.

The poet does not hoard what he discovers; having transcribed it, he soon loses it. In that resides his novelty, his infinity, his danger.

My skill is prow skill.

One is born with men, one dies unconsoled among the gods.

The earth that receives the grain is sad. The grain that will risk so much is happy.

There is a curse that resembles no other. It blinks in a lazy way, has an agreeable nature, puts on a reassuring face. But what resilience, once it has done with feinting, what a rush straight to the target! Probably, since the shadow in which it puts up its scaffolding is malignant and the region a dead secret, it will elude any name, will always escape in good time. It outlines, upon the sky veil

179

dessine dans le voile du ciel de quelques clairvoyants des paraboles assez effrayantes.

Livres sans mouvement. Mais livres qui s'introduisent avec souplesse dans nos jours, y poussent une plainte, ouvrent des bals.

Comment dire ma liberté, ma surprise, au terme de mille détours: il n'y a pas de fond, il n'y a pas de plafond.

Parfois la silhouette d'un jeune cheval, d'un enfant lointain, s'avance en éclaireur vers mon front et saute la barre de mon souci. Alors sous les arbres reparle la fontaine.

Nous désirons rester inconnus à la curiosité de celles qui nous aiment. Nous les aimons.

La lumière a un âge. La nuit n'en a pas. Mais quel fut l'instant de cette source entière?

Ne pas avoir plusieurs morts suspendues et comme enneigées. N'en avoir qu'une, de bon sable. Et sans résurrection.

Arrêtons-nous près des êtres qui peuvent se couper de leurs ressources, bien qu'il n'existe pour eux que peu ou pas de repli. L'attente leur creuse une insomnie vertigineuse. La beauté leur pose un chapeau de fleurs.

Oiseaux qui confiez votre gracilité, votre sommeil périlleux à un ramas de roseaux, le froid venu, comme nous vous ressemblons!

J'admire les mains qui emplissent, et, pour apparier, pour joindre, le doigt qui refuse le dé.

Je m'avise parfois que le courant de notre existence est peu saisissable, puisque nous subissons non seulement sa faculté capricieuse, mais le facile mouvement des bras et des jambes qui nous ferait aller là où nous serions heureux d'aller, sur la rive convoitée, à la rencontre d'amours of a few who are clear-sighted, some rather scaring parables.

Books without movement. Yet books that find their way lithely into our days, let fly a lamentation there, begin dances.

How find words for my liberty, my surprise, at the end of so many détours? There is no bottom, there is no ceiling.

Sometimes the silhouette of a colt, of a child in the distance, comes scouting toward my forehead and jumps the rail of my care. Then under the trees the fountain speaks again.

We long to remain unknown to the curiosity of the women who love us. We love them.

Light has age. Night has none. But what was the instant of this intact spring?

Not to have several deaths, suspended and as though snowed up. To have only one, of good sand. And without resurrection.

Let us stop close by those people who can cut themselves off from their resources, even if for them there is little or no leeway. Waiting digs in them a vertiginous insomnia. Beauty covers them with a hat of flowers.

Birds who entrust your slenderness, your perilous sleep to a shock of reeds, when the cold has come, how like you we are!

I admire the hands that fill and, for matching, for joining, the finger that refuses a thimble.

I notice sometimes that the current of our existence is hard to distinguish, because we are not only subject to its arbitrariness, but the easy movement of the arms and legs that would make us go where we would be glad to go, on the coveted bank, to meet loves whose differences would dont les différences nous enrichiraient, ce mouvement demeure inaccompli, vite déclinant en image, comme un parfum en boule sur notre pensée.

Désir, désir qui sait, nous ne tirons avantage de nos ténèbres qu'à partir de quelques souverainetés véritables assorties d'invisibles flammes, d'invisibles chaînes, qui, se révélant, pas après pas, nous font briller.

La beauté fait son lit sublime toute seule, étrangement bâtit sa renommée parmi les hommes, à côté d'eux mais à l'écart.

Semons les roseaux et cultivons la vigne sur les coteaux, au bord des plaies de notre esprit. Doigts cruels, mains précautionneuses, ce lieu facétieux est propice.

Celui qui invente, au contraire de celui qui découvre, n'ajoute aux choses, n'apporte aux êtres que des masques, des entre-deux, une bouillie de fer.

Enfin toute la vie, quand j'arrache la douceur de ta vérité amoureuse à ton profond!

Restez près du nuage. Veillez près de l'outil. Toute semence est détestée.

Bienfaisance des hommes certains matins stridents. Dans le fourmillement de l'air en délire, je monte, je m'enferme, insecte indévoré, suivi et poursuivant.

Face à ces eaux, de formes dures, où passent en bouquets éclatés toutes les fleurs de la montagne verte, les Heures épousent des dieux.

Frais soleil dont je suis la liane.

enrich us—this movement remains unachieved, quickly declining to an image, like a scent curled up on our thought.

Desire, desire aware, we gain advantage from our darkness only by having the use of certain true sovereignties matched with invisible flames, with invisible chains, which, revealing themselves, step by step, make us glitter.

Beauty makes her sublime bed all alone, builds her fame singularly among men, at their side yet apart.

Let us sow reeds and cultivate the vine on the hillslopes, fringing the wounds of our spirit. Cruel fingers, prudent hands, this humorous place is propitious.

The man who invents, unlike the one who discovers, adds to things, brings to human beings nothing but masks, middle ways, iron gruel.

Life at last whole, now that I wrench from your depth the sweetness of your living truth!

Stay near the cloud. Watch beside the tool. Every sowing is hated.

The good-will of men on strident mornings! In the swarming of the delirious air I rise up, I shut myself in, an undevoured insect, hunted and hunting.

Facing these waters, hard-shaped, into which there pass in burst bunches all the flowers of the green mountain, the Hours marry gods.

Cool sun whose climbing plant I am.

J.G.

183

Sur une nuit sans ornement

Regarder la nuit battue à mort; continuer à nous suffire en elle.

Dans la nuit, le poète, le drame et la nature ne font qu'un, mais en montée et s'aspirant.

La nuit porte nourriture, le soleil affine la partie nourrie.

Dans la nuit se tiennent nos apprentissages en état de servir à d'autres, après nous. Fertile est la fraîcheur de cette gardienne!

L'infini attaque mais un nuage sauve.

La nuit s'affilie à n'importe quelle instance de la vie disposée à finir en printemps, à voler par tempête.

La nuit se colore de rouille quand elle consent à nous entrouvrir les grilles de ses jardins.

Au regard de la nuit vivante, le rêve n'est parfois qu'un lichen spectral.

Il ne fallait pas embraser le cœur de la nuit. Il fallait que l'obscur fût maître où se cisèle la rosée du matin.

La nuit ne succède qu'à elle. Le beffroi solaire n'est qu'une tolérance intéressée de la nuit.

La reconduction de notre mystère, c'est la nuit qui en prend soin; la toilette des élus, c'est la nuit qui l'exécute.

La nuit déniaise notre passé d'homme, incline sa psyché devant le présent, met de l'indécision dans notre avenir.

Je m'emplirai d'une terre céleste.

Nuit plénière où le rêve malgracieux ne clignote plus, garde-moi vivant ce que j'aime.

On a Night Without Adornment

To gaze on night beaten to death; go on subsisting in her.

By night the poet, drama, and nature are one, but in the ascendant and breathing each other in.

Night brings nourishment, sun refines the part nourished.

By night our apprenticeships hold themselves ready to serve others, after us. Fertile is this guardian's coolness!

The infinite attacks but a cloud saves.

Night affiliates herself with any instance of life apt to end as spring, to fly by storm.

Night gets stained with rust when she consents to set ajar for us the wrought-iron gates of her gardens.

Seen against the living night, a dream is sometimes merely a ghostly lichen.

It was wrong to fire the heart of night. It was fitting that the dark be master where the morning dew is carved.

Night succeeds herself only. The solar belfry is merely a thing night tolerates for ends of her own.

Renewing the lease of our mystery is in night's care; robing the elect is night's work.

Night decants a man's past, subdues the psyche before the present, puts indecision into our future.

I'll fill myself with a celestial earth.

Plenary night where the uncouth dream no longer flickers, keep what I love alive for me.

J.G.

185

Pour un Prométhée saxifrage

En touchant la main éolienne de Hölderlin.

A Denise Naville.

La réalité sans l'énergie disloquante de la poésie, qu'est-ce?

Dieu avait trop puissamment vécu parmi nous. Nous ne savions plus nous lever et partir. Les étoiles sont mortes dans nos yeux, qui furent souveraines dans son regard.

Ce sont les questions des anges qui ont provoqué l'irruption des démons. Ils nous fixèrent au rocher, pour nous battre et pour nous aimer. De nouveau.

La seule lutte a lieu dans les ténèbres. La victoire n'est que sur leurs bords.

Noble semence, guerre et faveur de mon prochain, devant la sourde aurore je te garde avec mon quignon, attendant ce jour prévu de haute pluie, de limon vert, qui viendra pour les brûlants, et pour les obstinés.

Déclarer son nom

J'avais dix ans. La Sorgue m'enchâssait. Le soleil chantait les heures sur le sage cadran des eaux. L'insouciance et la douleur avaient scellé le coq de fer sur le toit des maisons et se supportaient ensemble. Mais quelle roue dans le cœur de l'enfant aux aguets tournait plus fort, tournait plus vite que celle du moulin dans son incendie blanc?

186

For a Saxifrage Prometheus
On touching the Aeolian hand of Hölderlin.

To Denise Naville.

What is reality without the dislocating energy of poetry?

God had lived among us too powerfully. We no longer knew how to rise and leave. The stars are dead in our eyes, after being sovereign in his gaze.

It was the questions of the angels that provoked the irruption of the demons. They shackled us to the rock, to beat us and to love us. Again.

The only struggle takes place in the dark. No victory except on its edge.

Noble sowing, my neighbor's war and favor, facing the muted dawn I keep you along with my hunk of bread, waiting for what I foresee as a day of tall rain, of green loam, which will come for those who burn, and for the stubborn.

J.G.

Declaring One's Name

I was ten. The Sorgue enshrined me. The sun was singing the hours on the wise clockface of the waters. Unconcern and grief had clamped the weathercock on the roofs of houses and bore with one another. But what wheel in the heart of the watchful child turned more forcefully, turned more quickly than that of the mill in its white consuming?

M.A.C.

187

La colline qu'il a bien servie descend en torrent dans son dos. Les langues pauvres le saluent; les mulets au pré lui font fête. La face rose de l'ornière tourne deux fois vers lui l'onde de son miroir. La méchanceté dort. Il est tel qu'il se rêvait.

The hill he has served so well descends torrential at his back. Poor tongues salute him; the mules in the meadow welcome him. The gulley's rose-hued face turns toward him twice the waters of its mirror. Meanness sleeps. He is as he dreamt himself to be.

M.A.C.

La faux relevée

Quand le bouvier des morts frappera du bâton,
Dédiez à l'été ma couleur dispersée.
Avec mes poings trop bleus étonnez un enfant.
Disposez sur ses joues ma lampe et mes épis.

Fontaine, qui tremblez dans votre étroit réduit,
Mon gain, aux soifs des champs, vous le prodiguerez.
De l'humide fougère au mimosa fiévreux,
Entre le vieil absent et le nouveau venu,
Le mouvement d'aimer, s'abaissant, vous dira:
«Hormis là, nul endroit, la disgrâce est partout.»

Scythe, Lifted Again

When the dead men's drover strikes with his rod,
Dedicate to summer my color dispersed.
Amaze a child with my fists too blue.
Arrange on his cheeks my lamp and my sheaves.

Fountain, trembling within your narrow nook,
My gain you'll spread bounteous to fields athirst.
From humid fern to fevered mimosa,
Between the aged absent and the new lately come,
The motion of loving, bending down, will tell you:
"Apart from there, nowhere, disgrace is on all sides."

M.A.C.

191

Contrevenir

Obéissez à vos porcs qui existent. Je me soumets à mes dieux qui n'existent pas.

Nous restons gens d'inclémence.

L'allégresse

Les nuages sont dans les rivières, les torrents parcourent le ciel. Sans saisie les journées montent en graine, meurent en herbe. Le temps de la famine et celui de la moisson, l'un sous l'autre dans l'air haillonneux, ont effacé leur différence. Ils filent ensemble, ils bivaquent! Comment la peur serait-elle distincte de l'espoir, passant raviné? Il n'y a plus de seuil aux maisons, de fumée aux clairières. Est tombé au gouffre le désir de chaleur—et ce peu d'obscurité dans notre dos où s'inquiétait la primevère dès qu'épiait l'avenir.

Pont sur la route des invasions, mentant au vainqueur, exorable au défait. Saurons-nous, sous le pied de la mort, si le cœur, ce gerbeur, ne doit pas précéder mais suivre?

192

Contravening

Obey your swine who exist. I submit to my gods who do not.

We remain men for inclemency.

M.A.C.

Gladness

Clouds are in the rivers, torrents course through the sky. Unpicked, the days rise and seed, perish in the green. The time of famine and the time of harvest, one beneath the other in the tattered air, have wiped out their difference. They slip by together, they encamp! How should fear be distinct from hope, furrowed passerby? No more threshold to the houses, nor smoke to the clearings. Fallen to the pit, the desire for warmth, and this slight darkness at our back where the primrose became restless at the future's peeping.

Bridge on the invader's path, deceptive to the victor, merciful to the undone. Shall we know, under the heel of death, if the heart, binder of sheaves, should not precede but follow?

M.A.C.

193

Fontis

Le raisin a pour patrie
Les doigts de la vendangeuse.
Mais elle, qui a-t-elle,
Passé l'étroit sentier de la vigne cruelle?

Le rosaire de la grappe;
Au soir le très haut fruit couchant qui saigne
La dernière étincelle.

Subsidence[10]

Grapes have for their homeland
The harvester's fingers.
But whom does she have
Past the cruel vine's narrow path?

The rosary of the cluster;
At evening, the lofty fruit setting, bleeding
The last spark.

M.A.C.

[10] The title "Fontis" is a geological term (thus "subsidence") but also a woman's name and a recollection of a fountain.

LE NU PERDU

1964-1970

NAKEDNESS LOST

1964-1970

Nous nous sentons complètement détachés d'Icare qui se voulut oiseau et de Léonard qui le poussa à l'être, bien que le second, avec un génie qui nous laissa de meilleures visions, naquit longtemps après que le premier fut revenu en purée de l'air du ciel. Nous resterons, pour vivre et mourir, avec les loups, *filialement, sur cette terre formicante. Ainsi nous désobéirons gaiement à l'inconscient prémoniteur qui nous incite, en nous vêtant d'oripeaux, à fuir cette rondeur trop éclairée qu'un cancer mortifie de ses mains savantes. Nous y sommes: malheureux et heureux, détruits et destructeurs, voraces de son allant, de ses épreuves, de ses éclats, de ses hasards, de sa parole et de son sol. La main de l'esprit est trop lasse, les rapports sont hypnotiques, et l'évasion est monotone.*

Retour amont *ne signifie pas retour aux sources. Il s'en faut. Mais saillie, retour aux aliments non différés de la source, et à son œil, amont, c'est-à-dire au pire lieu déshérité qui soit.*

We feel completely detached from Icarus who willed himself a bird and from Leonardo who drove him to it, although the latter, whose genius bequeathed us better visions, was born long after the former had returned, shattered from the high air. We shall remain, to live and to die, with the wolves, *filially, upon this teeming earth. Thus we shall merrily disobey the warning of our unconscious, which urges us, clothing us in tawdry garb, to flee this globe too brightly lit, which a cancer mortifies with its artful hands. Here we are: unhappy and content, destroyed and destructive, hungry for its pace, its trials, its flashes, its hazards, its speech, and its earth. The hand of the spirit is too weary, the relations are hypnotic, and evasion is monotonous.*

Returning Upland *does not mean a returning to the source. Far from it. Rather a sally, a returning to nourishment that has not been deferred from the source, and to its eye, upstream, that is, to the most forlorn place possible.*

M.A.C.

Tracé sur le gouffre

Dans la plaie chimérique de Vaucluse je vous ai regardé
souffrir. Là, bien qu'abaissé, vous étiez une eau verte, et
encore une route. Vous traversiez la mort en son désordre.
Fleur vallonnée d'un secret continu.

Chérir Thouzon

Lorsque la douleur l'eut hissé sur son toit envié un savoir
évident se montra à lui sans brouillard. Il ne se trouvait
plus dans sa liberté telles deux rames au milieu de l'océan.
L'ensorcelant désir de parole s'était, avec les eaux noires,
retiré. Çà et là persistaient de menus tremblements dont
il suivait le sillage aminci. Une colombe de granit à demi
masquée mesurait de ses ailes les restes épars du grand
œuvre englouti. Sur les pentes humides, la queue des
écumes et la course indigente des formes rompues. Dans
l'ère rigoureuse qui s'ouvrait, aboli serait le privilège de
récolter sans poison. Tous les ruisseaux libres et fous de
la création avaient bien fini de ruer. Au terme de sa vie il
devrait céder à l'audace nouvelle ce que l'immense pa-
tience lui avait, à chaque aurore, consenti. Le jour tour-
noyait sur Thouzon. La mort n'a pas comme le lichen
arasé l'espérance de la neige. Dans le creux de la ville
immergée, la corne de la lune mêlait le dernier sang et le
premier limon.

Traced upon the Abyss

In the chimerical wound of Vaucluse I watched you suffering. There, although subsided, you were green water, and yet a road. You traversed death in its disorder. Flower valleyed by a continuous secret.

M.A.C.

To Cherish Thouzon[11]

When grief had hoisted him onto its coveted roof, an obvious knowledge appeared to him with no mist. No longer did he find himself in his freedom like two oars in midocean. The captivating desire of the word had withdrawn, along with the black waters. Here and there persisted slight disturbances whose narrowed wake he followed. A granite dove half-masked measured with its wings the scattered remains of the great work engulfed. Over the damp slopes, the trailing of froth and the sparse flow of broken forms. In the rigorous era at its outset, the privilege of harvesting without poison would be abolished. All of creation's free and reckless rivers had done with their lashing. At his life's close he would cede to fresh audacity what boundless patience had granted him at each dawn. The day swirled over Thouzon. Death has not like the lichen worn down the expectation of snow. In the hollow of the immersed town, the moon's horn mingled last blood and first silt.

M.A.C.

[11] On a hill overlooking Le Thor are the ruins of a medieval monastery and a castle, refuge of the sect called the Cathars: the dove is a symbol of the early church. "Le grand oeuvre" may refer to the Cathars' work, to the building's fabric, and to alchemical transmutation.

Ils prennent pour de la clarté le rire jaune des ténèbres. Ils soupèsent dans leurs mains les restes de la mort et s'écrient: «Ce n'est pas pour nous.» Aucun viatique précieux n'embellit la gueule de leurs serpents déroulés. Leur femme les trompe, leurs enfants les volent, leurs amis les raillent. Ils n'en distinguent rien, par haine de l'obscurité. Le diamant de la création jette-t-il des feux obliques? Promptement un leurre pour le couvrir. Ils ne poussent dans leur four, ils n'introduisent dans la pâte lisse de leur pain qu'une pincée de désespoir fromental. Ils se sont établis et prospèrent dans le berceau d'une mer où l'on s'est rendu maître des glaciers. Tu es prévenu.

Comment, faible écolier, convertir l'avenir et détiser ce feu tant questionné, tant remué, tombé sur ton regard fautif?

Le présent n'est qu'un jeu ou un massacre d'archers.

Dès lors fidèle à son amour comme le ciel l'est au rocher. Fidèle, méché, mais sans cesse vaguant, dérobant sa course par toute l'étendue montrée du feu, tenue du vent; l'étendue, trésor de boucher, sanglante à un croc.

202

Mirage of the Peaks

They take for clarity the jaundiced laughter of shadows. They weigh in their hands death's remains and exclaim: "This is not for us." No precious viaticum embellishes the mouth of their uncoiled snakes. Their wife betrays them, their children rob them, their friends mock them. They see none of it, through hatred of darkness. Does creation's diamond cast oblique fires? Quickly a decoy to shroud it. They thrust in their oven, they place in the smooth dough of their bread just a small pinch of wheaten despair. They have settled and they prosper in the cradle of a sea where glaciers have been mastered. Be warned.

How may we, as a frail beginner, convert the future and rake out this fire interrogated and stirred up so often, which has caught on your offending gaze?

The present is only a game or a massacre of archers.

From then on faithful to his love as is the sky to the rock. Faithful, fused, but ceaselessly wandering, concealing his way through all the sweep revealed by the fire, held by the wind; the sweep, the butcher's hoard, bleeding on a hook.

M.A.C.

Aux portes d'Aerea

L'heureux temps. Chaque cité était une grande famille que la peur unissait; le chant des mains à l'œuvre et la vivante nuit du ciel l'illuminaient. Le pollen de l'esprit gardait sa part d'exil.

Mais le présent perpétuel, le passé instantané, sous la fatigue maîtresse, ôtèrent les lisses.

Marche forcée, au terme épars. Enfants battus, chaume doré, hommes sanieux, tous à la roue! Visée par l'abeille de fer, la rose en larmes s'est ouverte.

Devancier

J'ai reconnu dans un rocher la mort fuguée et mensurable, le lit ouvert de ses petits comparses sous la retraite d'un figuier. Nul signe de tailleur: chaque matin de la terre ouvrait ses ailes au bas des marches de la nuit.

Sans redite, allégé de la peur des hommes, je creuse dans l'air ma tombe et mon retour.

204

At the Gates of Aerea[12]

Happy times. Each city was one great family that fear kept united; the song of hands at work and the sky's living night lit it. The pollen of the spirit retained its share of exile.

But the perpetual present, the instantaneous past, under masterful exhaustion, removed the bindings.

Forced march, to the scattered ending. Whipped children, golden straw, men with saving sores, all to the wheel! Target of the iron bee, the rose in tears has opened.

J.G.

Forerunner

I have recognized, in a rock, death fugal and measurable, the open bed of its small assistants under the seclusion of a fig tree. No sign of a stone-cutter: each morning of the earth opened its wings at the foot of night's flight of steps.

Without repetition, freed from fear of men, I dig in the air my grave and my return.

J.G.

[12] Aerea is a lost Roman town, said by Pliny and Strabo to have been set high on a plateau between Orange and Avignon; some historians have placed it near the jagged peaks of the Dentelles de Montmirail.

Venasque

Les gels en meute vous rassemblent,
Hommes plus ardents que buisson;
Les longs vents d'hiver vous vont pendre.
Le toit de pierre est l'échafaud
D'une église glacée debout.

Venasque[13]

The frosts round up the pack of you,
Men who burn hotter than any bush;
Winter's long winds mean to hang you.
The stone roof is the scaffold
Of a church frozen standing.

J.G.

[13] Venasque, a small "perched" village in the Monts du Vaucluse, with a Romanesque church.

Je t'ai montré La Petite-Pierre, la dot de sa forêt, le ciel
   qui naît aux branches,
L'ampleur de ses oiseaux chasseurs d'autres oiseaux,
Le pollen deux fois vivant sous la flambée des fleurs,
Une tour qu'on hisse au loin comme la toile du corsaire,
Le lac redevenu le berceau du moulin, le sommeil d'un
   enfant.

Là où m'oppressa ma ceinture de neige,
Sous l'auvent d'un rocher moucheté de corbeaux,
J'ai laissé le besoin d'hiver.
Nous nous aimons aujourd'hui sans au-delà et sans lignée,
Ardents ou effacés, différents mais ensemble,
Nous détournant des étoiles dont la nature est de voler
   sans parvenir.

Le navire fait route vers la haute mer végétale.
Tous feux éteints il nous prend à son bord.
Nous étions levés dès avant l'aube dans sa mémoire.
Il abrita nos enfances, lesta notre âge d'or,
L'appelé, l'hôte itinérant, tant que nous croyons à
   sa vérité.

Alsace—That Part of the World

I showed you La Petite-Pierre, the dowry of its forest,
  the sky born at the tips of the branches,
The compass of its birds hunters of other birds,
The twice-living pollen under the flare of the flowers,
A tower they're hoisting in the distance like the pirate's
  canvas,
The lake once again the mill's cradle, a child's sleep.

There, where my belt of snow oppressed me,
Under the eave of a rock flecked with crows,
I've left the need for winter.
We love each other today with no beyond and no issue,
Ardent or effaced, different yet together,
Turning away from the stars whose nature is to fly and
  never arrive.

The ship is bound for the high sea's vegetation.
With all lights dowsed she takes us aboard.
We were up before dawn in her memory.
She sheltered our childhoods, ballasted our golden age,
There at our call, the traveling host, while we believe
  her truth.

J.G.

Dansons aux Baronnies

En robe d'olivier
                    l'Amoureuse
    avait dit:
                    Croyez à ma très enfantine fidélité.
                    Et depuis,
une vallée ouverte
                    une côte qui brille
un sentier d'alliance
                    ont envahi la ville
où la libre douleur est sous le vif de l'eau.

210

Let's Go Dance at Les Baronnies[14]

In olive-tree dress
               the Girl in Love
    had said:
           Trust my truly childlike faithfulness.
          And since then,
an open valley
             a gleaming coast
a path of assent
         have invaded the town
where free pain is under the quick of the water.

J.G.

---

[14] At Buis-les-Baronnies, with its square and its fountain, surrounded by hills terraced with olive orchards, an annual fair of lime-blossoms is held.

Possessions extérieures

Parmi tout ce qui s'écrit hors de notre attention, l'infini du ciel, avec ses défis, son roulement, ses mots innombrables, n'est qu'une phrase un peu plus longue, un peu plus haletante que les autres.

Nous la lisons en chemin, par fragments, avec des yeux usés ou naissants, et donnons à son sens ce qui nous semble irrésolu et en suspens dans notre propre signification. Ainsi trouvons-nous la nuit différente, hors de sa chair et de la nôtre, enfin solidairement endormie et rayonnante de nos rêves. Ceux-ci s'attendent, se dispersent sans se souffrir enchaînés. Ils ne cessent point de l'être.

Faction du muet

Les pierres se serrèrent dans le rempart et les hommes vécurent de la mousse des pierres. La pleine nuit portait fusil et les femmes n'accouchaient plus. L'ignominie avait l'aspect d'un verre d'eau.

Je me suis uni au courage de quelques êtres, j'ai vécu violemment, sans vieillir, mon mystère au milieu d'eux, j'ai frissonné de l'existence de tous les autres, comme une barque incontinente au-dessus des fonds cloisonnés.

212

Exterior Possessions

Among everything that writes itself beyond our notice, the sky's infinitude, with its challenges, its rumbling, its innumerable words, is only a sentence slightly longer, of quicker breath than others.

We read it on our way, in fragments, with eyes worn out or freshly born, lending to its sense what seems irresolute and suspended in our own meaning. So we find night distinct, outside its flesh and ours, solidly asleep and radiant with our dreams. These await each other, scatter while not suffering to be restrained. They do not cease to be so.

M.A.C.

Sentinel of the Mute

In the rampart the stones huddled together and men lived on the moss of stones. The dead of night carried a rifle and women no longer gave birth. Ignominy resembled a glass of water.

I have joined in the courage of a few beings, have lived violently, without growing older, my mystery in their midst, I have trembled at the existence of all the others like an incontinent boat above the partitioned depths.

M.A.C.

213

Yvonne

La soif hospitalière

Qui l'entendit jamais se plaindre?

Nulle autre qu'elle n'aurait pu boire sans mourir les
    quarante fatigues,
Attendre, loin devant, ceux qui viendront après;
De l'éveil au couchant sa manœuvre était mâle.

Qui a creusé le puits et hisse l'eau gisante
Risque son cœur dans l'écart de ses mains.

Yvonne[15]

Hospitable Thirst

Who heard her complain, ever?

No one except her could have drunk, and not died of it,
  the forty exhaustions,
Waited, far ahead, for those who will come after;
From waking till sundown her common task was male.

Whoever has dug the well and raises recumbent water
Risks his heart in the disjoining of his hands.

J.G.

[15] Yvonne Zervos, wife of Christian Zervos, editor of the *Cahiers d'art*, gathered about her poets and painters who were grateful for her help and particularly for her generous friendship; she died in 1970.

Le nu perdu

Porteront rameaux ceux dont l'endurance sait user la nuit
noueuse qui précède et suit l'éclair. Leur parole reçoit
existence du fruit intermittent qui la propage en se dilacé-
rant. Ils sont les fils incestueux de l'entaille et du signe,
qui élevèrent aux margelles le cercle en fleurs de la jarre
du ralliement. La rage des vents les maintient encore
dévêtus. Contre eux vole un duvet de nuit noire.

Célébrer Giacometti

En cette fin d'après-midi d'avril 1964 le vieil aigle despote,
le maréchal-ferrant agenouillé, sous le nuage de feu de
ses invectives (son travail, c'est-à-dire lui-même, il ne
cessa de le fouetter d'offenses), me découvrit, à même le
dallage de son atelier, la figure de Caroline, son modèle,
le visage peint sur toile de Caroline—après combien de
coups de griffes, de blessures, d'hématomes?—, fruit de
passion entre tous les objets d'amour, victorieux du faux
gigantisme des déchets additionnés de la mort, et aussi des
parcelles lumineuses à peine séparées, de nous autres, ses
témoins temporels. Hors de son alvéole de désir et de
cruauté. Il se réfléchissait, ce beau visage sans antan qui
allait tuer le sommeil, dans le miroir de notre regard,
provisoire receveur universel pour tous les yeux futurs.

216

Nakedness Lost

They will bear boughs, they whose endurance has learned to wear out the gnarled night which precedes and follows the flash. Their speech receives existence from the intermittent fruit that spreads it by tearing itself apart. They are the incestuous sons of the gash and of the sign, who raised on the well-rims the blossom circle of the jar of rallying. The winds' fury keeps them still unclothed. Against them there flies a down of black night.

J.G.

To Celebrate Giacometti

On that late afternoon in April 1964 the old despot eagle, the kneeling blacksmith, under the fire-cloud of his invectives (ceaselessly he lashed his work, that is himself, with insults), showed me, lying on his studio's tiled floor, the form of Caroline his model, Caroline's face painted on canvas—after how many claw-strokes, wounds, blows?—, fruit of passion among all objects of love, victorious over the false hyperbole of death's accumulated rubbish, as well as those barely separate parcels of light, the rest of us, his temporal witnesses. Outside his alveole of desire and cruelty. It was reflected, that fine face with no yesteryear and sure to kill sleep, in the mirror of our gaze, provisional universal receiver for all future eyes.

J.G.

217

Septentrion

—Je me suis promenée au bord de la Folie.—

Aux questions de mon cœur,
S'il ne les posait point,
Ma compagne cédait,
Tant est inventive l'absence.
Et ses yeux en décrue comme le Nil violet
Semblaient compter sans fin leurs gages s'allongeant
Dessous les pierres fraîches.

La Folie se coiffait de longs roseaux coupants.
Quelque part ce ruisseau vivait sa double vie.
L'or cruel de son nom soudain envahisseur
Venait livrer bataille à la fortune adverse.

Lied du figuier

Tant il gela que les branches laiteuses
Molestèrent la scie, se cassèrent aux mains.
Le printemps ne vit pas verdir les gracieuses.

Le figuier demanda au maître du gisant
L'arbuste d'une foi nouvelle.
Mais le loriot, son prophète,
L'aube chaude de son retour,
En se posant sur le désastre,
Au lieu de faim, périt d'amour.

218

Septentrion[16]

—I have been out walking on the bank of the Folie—

To my heart's questions,
Although it did not ask them,
The woman beside me submitted,
So inventive is absence.
And her eyes subsiding like the violet Nile
Seemed endlessly counting their earnings thinning out
Under the cool stones.

The Folie wore in her hair long cutting reeds.
Somewhere that brook was living its double life.
The cruel gold of its name, sudden invader,
Was coming to give battle to adverse fortune.

J.G.

The Fig-tree's Lied

It froze so hard, the milky branches
Harassed the saw, snapped in men's hands.
Spring did not see the gracious ones grow green.

The fig-tree asked the master of the recumbent
For the bush of a new faith.
But the oriole, its prophet,
The warm dawn of its homing,
In alighting on the disaster,
Instead of hunger, perished of love.

J.G.

[16] "Septentrion" can refer to an astral direction, and to a geographical north. The Folie is a tiny stream, so named for its "mad" or irregular course.

Le village vertical

Tels des loups ennoblis
Par leur disparition,
Nous guettons l'an de crainte
Et de libération.

Les loups enneigés
Des lointaines battues,
A la date effacée.

Sous l'avenir qui gronde,
Furtifs, nous attendons,
Pour nous affilier,
L'amplitude d'amont.

Nous savons que les Choses arrivent
Soudainement,
Sombres ou trop ornées.

Le dard qui liait les deux draps
Vie contre vie, clameur et mont,
Fulgura.

The Vertical Village

Like the wolves ennobled
By their vanishing
We lie in wait for the year of
Dread and liberation.

The snowed-in wolves
Of remote hunts
With the date effaced.

Under the rumbling future,
Furtive, we are waiting
For, to bring us together,
The upland amplitude.

We know that Things do happen
Suddenly,
Somber or too ornate.

The dart joining both sheets together,
Life against life, clamor and mountain,
Flashed.

J.G.

Le jugement d'octobre

Joue contre joue deux gueuses en leur détresse roidie;
La gelée et le vent ne les ont point instruites, les ont
    négligées;
Enfants d'arrière-histoire
Tombées des saisons dépassantes et serrées là debout.
Nulles lèvres pour les transposer, l'heure tourne.
Il n'y aura ni rapt, ni rancune.
Et qui marche passe sans regard devant elles, devant nous.
Deux roses perforées d'un anneau profond
Mettent dans leur étrangeté un peu de défi.
Perd-on la vie autrement que par les épines?
Mais par la fleur, les longs jours l'ont su!
Et le soleil a cessé d'être initial.
Une nuit, le jour bas, tout le risque, deux roses,
Comme la flamme sous l'abri, joue contre joue avec
    qui la tue.

222

October Judgment

Cheek to cheek two wretches in their stiffened distress;
Frost and wind have taught them nothing, have neglected
  them;
Daughters of remote history
Fallen from the rushing seasons and standing there
  huddled.
No lips to transpose them, time moves on.
There'll be no abduction, no rancor.
And anyone walking along passes by them, by us, without
  a glance.
Two roses perforated by a deep ring
Are putting into their quaintness a little defiance.
Does one lose life otherwise than by thorns?
By the flower, of course, as the long days have learned!
And the sun has ceased to be initial.
A night, day low, full risk, two roses,
Like the flame under cover, cheek by cheek with the
  creature who is killing her.

                                          J.G.

Il faut escalader beaucoup de dogmes et de glace pour jouer de bonheur et s'éveiller rougeur sur la pierre du lit.

Entre eux et moi il y eut longtemps comme une haie sauvage dont il nous était loisible de recueillir les aubépines en fleurs, et de nous les offrir. Jamais plus loin que la main et le bras. Ils m'aimaient et je les aimais. Cet obstacle *pour le vent* où échouait ma pleine force, quel était-il? Un rossignol me le révéla, et puis une charogne.

La mort dans la vie, c'est inalliable, c'est répugnant; la mort avec la mort, c'est approchable, ce n'est rien, un ventre peureux y rampe sans trembler.

J'ai renversé le dernier mur, celui qui ceinture les nomades des neiges, et je vois—ô mes premiers parents—l'été du chandelier.

Notre figure terrestre n'est que le second tiers d'une poursuite continue, un point, amont.

224

You have to scale many dogmas and a mountain of ice to happen on good luck and awaken, a blush on bed rock.

Between them and myself stretched for a long time a kind of untamed hedge where we were free to gather the flowering hawthorns and offer them to each other. Never farther than the hand and the arm. They loved me and I them. This obstacle *for the wind* where my full strength failed, what was it? A nightingale revealed it to me, and then a carcass.

Death in life can admit of no alloy, it is repugnant; death with death can be approached, is nothing, a cowardly stomach crawls over it without trembling.

I have demolished the last wall, which girds the snow wanderers, and I behold—oh my first parents—the chandelier's summer.

Our earthly face is only the second third of a continuous pursuit, a point, upland.

M.A.C.

225

Le banc d'ocre

Par une terre d'Ombre et de rampes sanguines nous retournions aux rues. Le timon de l'amour ne nous dépassait pas, ne gagnait plus sur nous. Tu ouvris ta main et m'en montras les lignes. Mais la nuit s'y haussait. Je déposai l'infime ver luisant sur le tracé de vie. Des années de gisant s'éclairèrent soudain sous ce fanal vivant et altéré de nous.

Lutteurs

Dans le ciel des hommes, le pain des étoiles me sembla ténébreux et durci, mais dans leurs mains étroites je lus la joute de ces étoiles en invitant d'autres: émigrantes du pont encore rêveuses; j'en recueillis la sueur dorée, et par moi la terre cessa de mourir.

226

The Ochre Seam

Over an earth of Umber and of sanguine slopes we were
returning to roads. Love's tiller was not outstripping us,
was no longer gaining on us. You opened your hand and
showed me its map. But night was rising there. I laid'the
tiny glow-worm on the line of life. Years of recumbency
lit up suddenly under that living lantern thirsty for us.

M.A.C.

Wrestlers

In the sky of men, the star's bread seemed to me shadowy
and hardened, but in their narrow hands I read the joust
of these stars calling others: emigrants from below deck
still dreaming; I gathered their golden sweat, and through
me the earth ceased to die.

M.A.C.

Déshérence

La nuit était ancienne
Quand le feu l'entrouvrit.
Ainsi de ma maison.

On ne tue point la rose
Dans les guerres du ciel.
On exile une lyre.

Mon chagrin persistant,
D'un nuage de neige
Obtient un lac de sang.
Cruauté aime vivre.

O source qui mentis
A nos destins jumeaux,
J'élèverai du loup
Ce seul portrait pensif!

Default of Heirs

The night was old always
When fire set it ajar.
So with my house.

One never kills the rose
In the sky's wars of the sky.
One does exile a lyre.

My persistent grief
Out of a snow cloud
Obtains a lake of blood.
Cruelty likes to live.

Oh spring who gave the lie
To our twin destinies,
Of the wolf I shall raise
This sole pensive likeness.

J.G.

229

Bout des solennités

Affermi par la bonté d'un fruit hivernal, je rentrai le feu
dans la maison. La civilisation des orages gouttait à la
génoise du toit. Je pourrai à loisir haïr la tradition, rêver
au givre des passants sur des sentiers peu vétilleux. Mais
confier à qui mes enfants jamais nés? La solitude était
privée de ses épices, la flamme blanche s'enlisait, n'offrant
de sa chaleur que le geste expirant.

Sans solennité je franchis ce monde muré: j'aimerai
sans manteau ce qui tremblait sous moi.

Le gaucher

On ne se console de rien lorsqu'on marche en tenant une
main, la périlleuse floraison de la chair d'une main.

L'obscurcissement de la main qui nous presse et nous
entraîne, innocente aussi, l'odorante main où nous nous
ajoutons et gardons ressource, ne nous évitant pas le
ravin et l'épine, le feu prématuré, l'encerclement des
hommes, cette main préférée à toutes, nous enlève à la
duplication de l'ombre, au jour du soir. Au jour brillant
au-dessus du soir, froissé son seuil d'agonie.

End of Solemnities

Strengthened by the goodness of a winter fruit, I carried the fire into the house. The civilization of storms formed drop by drop at the roof's tiled eaves. I shall be able at leisure to hate tradition, to dream of the frost of passersby on paths not particular. But to whom might I entrust my children never born? Solitude was stripped of its spices, the white flame mired down, offering from its heat only the expiring gesture.

Without ceremony, I step across this walled-up world: I shall love uncloaked what was trembling under me.

M.A.C.

The Left-handed

You find consolation in nothing when you walk with a hand in yours, the perilous flowering of a hand's flesh.

The darkening of the hand urging us and drawing us along, innocent also, the fragrant hand where we are increased and keep our resource, not sparing us ravine and thorn, the premature fire, the encircling of men, this hand preferred to all others, removes us from the duplication of shadow, from the evening's day. From the day shining over the evening, its threshold of agony crumpled.

M.A.C.

L'ouest derrière soi perdu

L'ouest derrière soi perdu, présumé englouti, touché de rien, hors-mémoire, s'arrache à sa couche elliptique, monte sans s'essouffler, enfin se hisse et rejoint. Le point fond. Les sources versent. Amont éclate. Et en bas le delta verdit. Le chant des frontières s'étend jusqu'au belvédère d'aval. Content de peu est le pollen des aulnes.

The west lost behind you, assumed to have been engulfed, affected by nothing, out of memory, breaks away from its elliptical bed, rises without losing breath, hoists itself up at last and catches up. The point melts. The springs pour out. Upland bursts forth. And below, the delta turns green. The frontier song reaches to the vantage point of downstream. Easily contented is the alders' pollen.

M.A.C.

Où passer nos jours à présent?
Parmi les éclats incessants de la hache devenue folle à son tour?
Demeurons dans la pluie giboyeuse et nouons notre souffle à elle. Là, nous ne souffrirons plus rupture, dessèchement ni agonie; nous ne sèmerons plus devant nous notre contradiction renouvelée, nous ne sécrèterons plus la vacance où s'engouffrait la pensée, mais nous maintiendrons ensemble sous l'orage à jamais habitué, nous offrirons à sa brouillonne fertilité, les puissants termes ennemis, afin que buvant à des sources grossies ils se fondent en un inexplicable limon.

Where shall we spend our days at present?
Among the incessant sparks of the axe crazed in its turn?
Let us stay in the quarried rain and join to it our breathing.
No longer shall we suffer any rupture there, desiccation, or
the pangs of death; no longer shall we sow before us our re-
newed contradictions, no longer secrete the void where
thought rushed in, but we shall hold together under the storm
become forever familiar, shall offer to its confused fertility,
these powerful warring opposites, that, drinking at swollen
springs they may fuse in an inexplicable loam.

M.A.C.

D'un même lien

Atome égaré, arbrisseau,
Tu grandis, j'ai droit de parcours.
A l'enseigne du pré qui boit,
Peu instruits nous goûtions, enfants,
De pures clartés matinales.
L'amour qui prophétisa
Convie le feu à tout reprendre.

O fruit envolé de l'érable
Ton futur est un autrefois.
Tes ailes sont flammes défuntes,
Leur morfil amère rosée.
Vient la pluie de résurrection!
Nous vivons, nous, de ce loisir,
Lune et soleil, frein ou fouet,
Dans un ordre halluciné.

With One and the Same Bond

Atom astray, young tree,
You're growing tall, I have right of way.
At the sign of the drinking field
We, children, untaught, used to taste
Pure early-morning radiances.
Love that uttered prophecy
Invites fire to take all back.

Oh fruit flown from the maple, your
Future's once upon a time.
Your wings are exanimate flames,
Their leading edge a bitter dew.
At hand, the resurrection rain!
We—we are living on this leisure,
Moon and sun, bridle or whip,
In a hallucinated order.

J.G.

Tables de longévité

En la matière sèche du temps qui avant de nous anéantir déjà nous décime, ceux qui ont donné la mort expient en donnant le bonheur, un bonheur qu'ils n'éprouvent ni ne partagent. Ils n'ont à eux que le feu d'un mot inaltérable courant dans le dos de l'abîme et mal résigné à la fantasque oppression. La balance d'airain consentirait-elle à les remettre à l'innocence, que l'hôte auquel ils appartiennent les distinguerait encore là, nus, destitués, fascinants, dans l'incapacité de jouir du mot virtuel.

Quand il y a de moins en moins d'espace entre l'infini et nous, entre le soleil libertaire et le soleil procureur, nous sommes sur le banc de la nuit.

La cloche du pur départ ne tinte qu'en pays incréé ou follement agonisant.

L'âge d'or n'était qu'un crime différé.

Fugitifs qui tournent en ignorant leur parabole.

Nous ne sommes pas assez lents ni écartés du feu ancien pour atteler nos vérités à leur démence.

Souvenez-vous de cet homme comme d'un bel oiseau sans tête, aux ailes tendues dans le vent. Il n'est qu'un serpent à genoux.

238

*In the dry stuff of time that before annihilating us deci-
mates us, those who have dealt death expiate by dealing
happiness, a happiness they do not experience or share.
They themselves have merely the fire of a resistant word
running along the back of the abyss and imperfectly re-
signed to the whims of oppression. If the brazen balance
did restore them to innocence, the host they belong to
would pick them out still there, naked, destitute, casting a
spell, incapable of enjoying the word's potential.*

When there is less and less space between the infinite
and us, between the libertarian sun and the prosecutor sun,
we are aground on night.

The bell of pure departure tolls only in an uncreated or
a wildly agonizing country.

The golden age was simply a postponed crime.

Fugitives who twist and turn, not knowing their parable.

We are not slow enough or removed from the ancient
fire to harness our truths to their madness.

Remember this man as a fine bird with no head, its
wings outstretched in the wind. He is only a kneeling ser-
pent.

J.G.

239

Ces certitudes *distraites*, elles sont nos fondations. Nous ne pouvons les nommer, les produire et encore moins les céder. Sont-elles antérieures à nous? Datent-elles d'avant la parole et d'avant la peur? Et vont-elles cesser avec nous? A la fourche de notre branche, une toute récente sève les attend pour les saisir et pour les confirmer.

Quelques êtres ne sont ni dans la société ni dans une rêverie. Ils appartiennent à un destin isolé, à une espérance inconnue. Leurs actes apparents semblent antérieurs à la première inculpation du temps et à l'insouciance des cieux. Nul ne s'offre à les appointer. L'avenir fond devant leur regard. Ce sont les plus nobles et les plus inquiétants.

Cahier des émeutes, le cœur nourrit ce qu'il éclaire et reçoit de ce qu'il sert le cintre de sa rougeur. Mais l'espace où il s'incorpore lui est chaque nuit plus hostile. O la percutante, la ligneuse douleur!

Bientôt on ne voit plus mourir mais naître et grandir. Nos yeux sous notre front ont passé. Par contre, les yeux dans notre dos sont devenus immenses. La roue et son double horizon, l'un à présent très large et l'autre inexistant, vont achever leur tour.

Si l'on ne peut informer l'avenir à l'aide d'une grande bataille, il faut laisser des traces de combat. Les vraies victoires ne se remportent qu'à long terme et le front contre la nuit.

Méfiez-vous de moi comme je me méfie de moi, car je ne suis pas sans recul.

Nous avons les mains libres pour unir en un nouveau contrat la gerbe et la disgrâce dépassées. Mais la lenteur, la sanguinaire lenteur, autant que le pendule emballé, sur quels doigts se sont-ils rejoints?

Assessment

These *diverted* certainties are our foundations. We cannot name them, produce them, still less give them up. Do they pre-date us? Do they originate before the word and before fear? And will they cease with us? At the forking of our branch, a quite recent sap awaits them, to grasp and confirm them.

A few beings are neither in society nor in a state of dreaming. They belong to an isolated fate, to an unknown hope. Their open acts seem anterior to time's first inculpation and to the skies' unconcern. It occurs to no one to employ them. The future melts before their gaze. They are the noblest and the most disquieting.

Notebook of uprisings, the heart nourishes what it enlightens and receives from what it serves its crimson curve. But the space with which it merges shows more hostility each night. Oh ligneous grief, resounding!

Soon we see dying no longer but rather birth and increase. Our eyes have dimmed beneath our foreheads. However, our eyes looking back have grown immense. The wheel and its double horizon, one now wide of span and the other non-existent, are about to end their turning.

If we cannot mold the future by a great battle, we must leave traces of combat. True victories are won only over a long time, our forehead against the night.

Mistrust me as I mistrust myself, for I am not without recoil.

We have our hands free to unite in a new contract the sheaf and the disgrace exceeded. But deliberation, sanguinary deliberation, as well as the runaway pendulum, on what fingers have they joined?

M.A.C.

241

Sortie

Ineffable rigueur
Qui maintint nos vergers,
Dors mais éveille-moi.

C'était, ce sera
La lune de silex,
Un quartier battant l'autre,
Tels les amants unis
Que nous répercutons
En mille éclats distants.

Qui supporte le mal
Sous ses formes heureuses?
Fin de règne:
Levée des jeunesses.

Ineffable rigueur
Qui maintint nos vergers,
Tout offrir c'est jaillir de toi.

Exit

Ineffable severeness
That maintained our orchards,
Sleep but waken me.

It was, it will be
The flint moon, one
Quarter striking the next,
Like the united lovers
We reverberate
To a thousand distant flashes.

Who now endures evil
Under its happy forms?
End of reign:
Youth rising.

Ineffable severeness
That maintained our orchards,
To offer all is to spring from you.

J.G.

Tradition du météore

Espoir que je tente
La chute me boit.

Où la prairie chante
Je suis, ne suis pas.

Les étoiles mentent
Aux cieux qui m'inventent.

Nul autre que moi
Ne passe par là,

Sauf l'oiseau de nuit
Aux ailes traçantes.

*

Pâle chair offerte
Sur un lit étroit.

Aigre chair défaite,
Sombre au souterrain.

Reste à la fenêtre
Où ta fièvre bat,

O cœur volontaire,
Coureur qui combats!

Sur le gel qui croît,
Tu es immortel.

Hope I am tempting
Fall is drinking me.

Where the meadow sings
I am, I am not.

The stars tell lies
To the skies inventing me.

None other than me
Passes that way,

But this bird of night
With wings that leave wakes.

*

Pale flesh tendered
On a narrow bed.

Sour flesh surrendered,
Sink below ground.

Stay at the window
Where your fever throbs,

Oh wilful heart,
Runner embattled!

On the sprouting frost
You are immortal.

J.G.

Jeu muet

Avec mes dents
J'ai pris la vie
Sur le couteau de ma jeunesse.
Avec mes lèvres aujourd'hui,
Avec mes lèvres seulement . . .

Courte parvenue,
La fleur des talus,
Le dard d'Orion,
Est réapparu.

Mute Game

With my teeth
I have seized life
Up against my youth's knife.
With my lips today,
With my lips only.

The short-reaching
Flower of the roadsides,
Orion's dart,[17]
Has reappeared.

J.G.

[17] A small flower that releases its petals all at once.

Rémanence

De quoi souffres-tu? Comme si s'éveillait dans la maison sans bruit l'ascendant d'un visage qu'un aigre miroir semblait avoir figé. Comme si, la haute lampe et son éclat abaissés sur une assiette aveugle, tu soulevais vers ta gorge serrée la table ancienne avec ses fruits. Comme si tu revivais tes fugues dans la vapeur du matin à la rencontre de la révolte tant chérie, elle qui sut, mieux que toute tendresse, te secourir et t'élever. Comme si tu condamnais, tandis que ton amour dort, le portail souverain et le chemin qui y conduit.

De quoi souffres-tu?

De l'irréel intact dans le réel dévasté. De leurs détours aventureux cerclés d'appels et de sang. De ce qui fut choisi et ne fut pas touché, de la rive du bond au rivage gagné, du présent irréfléchi qui disparaît. D'une étoile qui s'est, la folle, rapprochée et qui va mourir avant moi.

248

From what do you suffer? As if in the noiseless house there were to awake the ascendancy of a face that an acrid mirror seemed to have fixed. As if, the high lamp and its radiance inclined over a blind plate, you were to lift toward your anguished throat the old table with its fruits. As if you were reliving your escapades in the morning haze toward the beloved revolt, which better than all tenderness, could succor you and raise you. As if condemning, while your love sleeps, the sovereign portal and the path leading toward it.

From what do you suffer?

From the unreal intact in the reality laid waste. From their venturesome deviations circled with cries and blood. From that which was chosen and left untouched, from the shore of the leap to the coast attained, from the unreflecting present that disappears. From a star which, foolish, came close and will die before me.

M.A.C.

Cours des argiles

Vois bien, portier aigu, du matin au matin,
Longues, lovant leur jet, les ronces frénétiques,
La terre nous presser de son regard absent,
La douleur s'engourdir, grillon au chant égal,
Et un dieu ne saillir que pour gonfler la soif
De ceux dont la parole aux eaux vives s'adresse.

Dès lors réjouis-toi, chère, au destin suivant:
Cette mort ne clôt pas la mémoire amoureuse.

Course of Clays

Watch, acute porter, morning to morning
Long, coiling their jets, the frantic brambles,
The land pressing us with its absent gaze,
The ache growing numb, a cricket's level song,
And a god springing only to swell the thirst
Of those whose speech is addressed to living waters.

Then rejoice, dearest, in the fate following:
This death does not end memory in love.

J.G.

Dyne

Passant l'homme extensible et l'homme transpercé, j'arrivai devant la porte de toutes les allégresses, celle du Verbe descellé de ses restes mortels, faisant du neuf, du feu avec la vérité, et fort de ma verte créance je frappai.

Ainsi atteindras-tu au pays lavé et désert de ton défi. Jusque-là, sans calendrier, tu l'édifieras. Sévère vanité! Mais qui eût parié et opté pour toi, des sites immémoriaux à la lyre fugitive du père?

Bienvenue

Ah! que tu retournes à ton désordre, et le monde au sien. L'asymétrie est jouvence. On ne garde l'ordre que le temps d'en haïr l'état de pire. Alors en toi s'excitera le désir de l'avenir, et chaque barreau de ton échelle inoccupée et tous les traits refoulés de ton essor te porteront, t'élèveront d'un même sentiment joyeux. Fils de l'ode fervente, tu abjureras la gigantesque moisissure. Les solstices fixent la douleur diffuse en un dur joyau diamantin. L'enfer à leur mesure que les râpeurs de métaux s'étaient taillé, redescendra vaincu dans son abîme. Devant l'oubli nouveau, le seul nuage au ciel sera le soleil.

Mentons en espoir à ceux qui nous mentent: que l'immortalité inscrite soit à la fois la pierre et la leçon.

252

Dyne

Passing man expandable and man pierced through, I arrived at the door of all gladness, of the Word unsealed from its mortal remains, making afresh, making fire from truth, and strong in my green credence, I knocked.

Thus will you attain the cleansed and desert country of your challenge. Until then, with no calendar, you will construct it. Austere vanity! But who would have wagered and chosen for you, from the sites immemorial to the father's fugitive lyre.

M.A.C.

Welcome

Ah! may you return to your disorder, and the world to its. Asymmetry is youthfulness. One maintains order just long enough to hate its becoming worse. Then in you the desire of the future will quicken, and every rung of the unoccupied ladder and all the repressed leaps of your soaring will carry you, will lift you in one same joyous emotion. Son of the fervent ode, you will abjure the giant mildew. The solstices will fix the diffused grief as a hard diamantine jewel. The hell to their scale, which the metal-filers had carved for themselves, will redescend conquered into its abyss. Before the new oblivion, the sole cloud in the sky will be the sun.

Let us tell lies, hoping, to those who lie to us: may inscribed immortality be at once the stone and the lesson.

J.G.

Permanent invisible

Permanent invisible aux chasses convoitées,
Proche, proche invisible et si proche à mes doigts,
O mon distant gibier la nuit où je m'abaisse
Pour un novice corps à corps.
Boire frileusement, être brutal répare.
Sur ce double jardin s'arrondit ton couvercle.
Tu as la densité de la rose qui se fera.

Enduring Invisible

Enduring invisible within coveted hunts,
Near, near invisible and so near my hand,
Oh my far-off prey the night where I stoop
For a novice wrestling.
To drink shivering, to be brutal restores you.
On this double garden arches your cover.
Yours is the density of the rose in its making.

M.A.C.

Les civilisations sont des graisses. L'Histoire échoue, Dieu faute de Dieu n'enjambe plus nos murs soupçonneux, l'homme feule à l'oreille de l'homme, le Temps se fourvoie, la fission est en cours. Quoi encore?

La science ne peut fournir à l'homme dévasté qu'un phare aveugle, une arme de détresse, des outils sans légende. Au plus dément: le sifflet de manœuvres.

Ceux qui ont installé l'éternel compensateur, comme finalité triomphale du temporel, n'étaient que des geôliers de passage. Ils n'avaient pas surpris la nature tragique, intervallaire, saccageuse, comme en suspens, des humains.

Lumière pourrissante, l'obscurité ne serait pas la pire condition.

Il n'y avait qu'une demi-liberté. Tel était l'octroi extrême. Demi-liberté pour l'homme en mouvement. Demi-liberté pour l'insecte qui dort et attend dans la chrysalide. Fantôme, tout juste souvenir, la liberté dans l'émeute. La liberté était au sommet d'une masse d'obéissances dissimulées et de conventions acceptées sous les traits d'un leurre irréprochable.

La liberté se trouve dans le cœur de celui qui n'a cessé de la vouloir, de la rêver, l'a obtenue contre le crime.

The Disdained Apparitions

Civilizations are sebaceous. History runs aground, God for lack of God no longer bestrides our suspicious walls, man roars in man's ear, time is astray, fission in progress. What besides?

Science can supply scorched earth man with only a blind light-house, an emergency weapon, tools without legend. To the maddest: the shunting-whistle.

Those who installed the eternal compensator as a teleology to confound the temporal were merely transient jailers. They had not penetrated the nature, tragic, full of gaps, havoc-making, as though in abeyance, of human beings.

Rotting light, darkness would not be the worst fate.

There was only a half-liberty. That was the utmost allowance. Half-liberty for man on the move. Half-liberty for the insect asleep and waiting in the chrysalis. A phantom, a memory if that, liberty in a riot. Liberty was at the summit of a mass of concealed obediences and of conventions accepted under the features of some irreproachable decoy.

Liberty is to be found in the heart of the man who has not ceased willing, dreaming, has won it in exchange for crime.

J.G.

De même qu'il y a plusieurs nuits différentes dans l'espace, il y a plusieurs dieux sur les plages du jour. Mais ils sont si étalés qu'entre souffle et ressaut une vie s'est passée.

Les dieux ne déclinent ni ne meurent, mais par un mouvoir impérieux et cyclique, comme l'océan, se retirent. On ne les approche, parmi les trous d'eau, qu'ensevelis.

Meilleur fils du vieux disque solaire et au plus près de sa céleste lenteur. Cette envie substantielle se répéta, se répéta, puis sa tache se perdit.

Nuit à loisir recerclée, qui *nous* joue?

Even If . . .

Just as there are several different nights in space, there are several gods on the shores of day. But they are so spread out that between breath and springing a life has gone by.

The gods do nct decline nor do they die, but with an imperious and cyclical movement, like the ocean, they withdraw. You approach them only among the water-holes, buried.

Best child of the old solar disk and nearest to its celestial slowness. This substantial longing came again, came again, then its spot vanished.

Night at leisure re-hooped, who plays *us*?

J.G.

Le pays natal est un allié diminué. Sinon il nous entretiendrait de ses revers et de sa fatuité.

Pistes, sentiers, chemins et routes ne s'accordent pas sur les mêmes maisons, choisissent d'autres habitants, rendent compte à des yeux différents.

La question à se poser sans cesse: par où et comment rendre la nuit du rêve aux hommes? Et pour tromper l'horreur dont ils sont visités: à l'aide de quelle matière surnaturelle, de quel futur et millénaire amour?

Ne pas donner à l'oiseau plus d'ailes qu'il n'en peut. Pour son malheur il nous égalerait.

Dans les lieux d'épouvante qu'il s'apprête à conquérir, l'orgueilleux se fait précéder d'une fusée. Le désespoir aussi. Sans lustre.

One's native country is a diminished ally. Otherwise it would leave us no rest from its setbacks and its fatuity.

Tracks, paths, roads, and highways do not agree on the same houses, they choose other inhabitants, are accountable to different pairs of eyes.

The question to ask oneself and never cease: from where and how to restore to men the night of dreaming? And to cheat the horror that visits them: with the aid of what supernatural material, of what future and millennium-lasting love?

Never give the bird more wings than he can carry. To his own misfortune he would be our equal.

In those places of terror he is preparing to conquer, the proud man has a rocket go before him. Despair, too. Unshining.

J.G.

261

Nous avons répété tout seuls la leçon de vol de nos parents. Leur hâte à se détacher de nous n'avait d'égal que leur fièvre à se retrouver deux, à redevenir le couple impérieux qu'ils semblaient former à l'écart; et rien que lui. Abandon à nos chances, à leur contraire? Eux partis, nous nous rendîmes compte qu'au lieu de nous lancer vers l'avant, leur leçon enflammait nos faiblesses, portait sur des points dont la teneur, d'un temps à un autre, avait changé. L'art qui naît du besoin, à la seconde où le besoin en est distrait, est un vivre concordant entre la montagne et l'oiseau.

Good Neighbors

We have practiced on our own the lesson in flight our parents gave us. Their hurry to detach themselves from us was equal only to their fever to be again two, to become again the imperious couple they seemed to form apart; that and nothing else. Abandonment to our chances, to their opposite? With them gone we realized that, instead of launching us forward, their lesson was inflaming our weaknesses, was bearing on points whose meaning, in the course of time, had changed. Art that is born of need, at the second when need is diverted from it, is concordant living between mountain and bird.

J.G.

Contre une maison sèche

S'il te faut repartir, prends appui contre une maison sèche. N'aie point souci de l'arbre grâce auquel, de très loin, tu la reconnaîtras. Ses propres fruits le désaltèreront.

Levé avant son sens, un mot nous éveille, nous prodigue la clarté du jour, un mot qui n'a pas rêvé.

*

Espace couleur de pomme. Espace, brûlant compotier.

Aujourd'hui est un fauve. Demain verra son bond.

*

Mets-toi à la place des dieux et regarde-toi. Une seule fois en naissant échangé, corps sarclé où l'usure échoue, tu es plus invisible qu'eux. Et tu te répètes moins.

La terre a des mains, la lune n'en a pas. La terre est meurtrière, la lune désolée.

*

La liberté c'est *ensuite* le vide, un vide à désespérément recenser. Après, chers emmurés éminentissimes, c'est la forte odeur de votre dénouement. Comment vous surprendrait-elle?

Faut-il l'aimer ce nu altérant, lustre d'une vérité au cœur sec, au sang convulsif!

*

Avenir déjà raturé! Monde plaintif!

Quand le masque de l'homme s'applique au visage de la terre, elle a les yeux crevés.

*

Against a Dry House

If you must set out again, prop yourself against a dry house. Never worry about the tree by whose help, from far off, you will recognize it. The tree's own fruits will slake its thirst.

Risen before its meaning, a word wakes us, lavishes on us the brightness of day, a word that has not dreamed.

*

Space apple-colored. Space, burning fruit-dish.

Today is a wild beast. Tomorrow will see its leap.

*

Put yourself in the place of the gods and look at yourself. Just once, exchanged at birth, a weeded body where attrition fails, you are more invisible than they are. And you repeat yourself less.

The earth has hands, the moon has none. The earth is murderous, the moon ravaged.

*

Liberty, *next*, is emptiness, an emptiness to be desperately surveyed. Later, dear people and most eminent immured ones, comes the strong smell of your unraveling. Should that surprise you?

One has to love that parching nakedness, lustre of a hard hearted, convulsive blooded truth!

*

Future already deleted! Plaintive world!

When man's mask is clapped onto the earth's face, she has her eyes put out.

*

Sommes-nous hors de nos gonds pour toujours? Repeints d'une beauté sauve?

J'aurais pu prendre la nature comme partenaire et danser avec elle à tous les bals. Je l'aimais. Mais deux ne s'épousent pas aux vendanges.

*

Mon amour préférait le fruit à son fantôme. J'unissais l'un à l'autre, insoumis et courbé.

Trois cent soixante-cinq nuits sans les jours, bien massives, c'est ce que je souhaite aux haïsseurs de la nuit.

*

Ils vont nous faire souffrir, mais nous les ferons souffrir. Il faudrait dire à l'or qui roule: «Venge-toi.» Au temps qui désunit: «Serai-je avec qui j'aime? O, ne pas qu'entrevoir!»

Sont venus des tranche-montagnes qui n'ont que ce que leurs yeux saisissent pour eux. Individus prompts à terroriser.

*

N'émonde pas la flamme, n'écourte pas la braise en son printemps. Les migrations, par les nuits froides, ne s'arrêteraient pas à ta vue.

Nous éprouvons les insomnies du Niagara et cherchons des terres émues, des terres propres à émouvoir une nature à nouveau enragée.

Le peintre de Lascaux, Giotto, Van Eyck, Uccello, Fouquet, Mantegna, Cranach, Carpaccio, Georges de La Tour, Poussin, Rembrandt, laines de mon nid rocheux.

*

266

Are we off our hinges for ever? Repainted with a scatheless beauty?

I could have taken Nature as my partner and danced with her at every outing. I loved her. But couples don't get married at harvestings.

*

My love preferred the fruit to its phantom. I joined them together. I was unsubdued and bowed.

Three hundred and sixty-five nights without their days, real massive ones, is what I wish the haters of night.

*

They are going to make us suffer, but we shall make them suffer. One should say to the gold as it rolls: "Avenge yourself." To time that disunites: "Shall I be with the one I love? Oh, to do more than glimpse!"

There have come swaggerers who have only what their eyes seize for them. Individuals all set to terrorize.

*

Don't prune the flame, don't curtail the ember in its spring-time. The migrations, on cold nights, would not stop at the sight of you.

We are going through the insomnias of Niagara and searching for stirred lands, for lands fit to stir a nature once more enraged.

The Lascaux painter, Giotto, Van Eyck, Uccello, Fouquet, Mantegna, Cranach, Carpaccio, Georges de La Tour, Poussin, Rembrandt, wools lining my rock nest.

*

267

Nos orages nous sont essentiels. Dans l'ordre des douleurs la société n'est pas fatalement fautive, malgré ses étroites places, ses murs, leur écroulement et leur restauration alternés.

On ne peut se mesurer avec l'image qu'autrui se fait de nous, l'analogie bientôt se perdrait.

*

Nous passerons de la mort imaginée aux roseaux de la mort vécue nûment. La vie, par abrasion, se distrait à travers nous.

La mort ne se trouve ni en deçà, ni au delà. Elle est à côté, industrieuse, infime.

*

Je suis né et j'ai grandi parmi des contraires tangibles à tout moment, malgré leurs exactions spacieuses et les coups qu'ils se portaient. Je courus les gares.

Cœur luisant n'éclaire pas que sa propre nuit. Il redresse le peu agile épi.

*

Il en est qui laissent des poisons, d'autres des remèdes. Difficiles à déchiffrer. Il faut goûter.

Le oui, le non immédiats, c'est salubre en dépit des corrections qui vont suivre.

*

Au séjour supérieur, nul invité, nul partage: l'urne fondamentale. L'éclair trace le présent, en balafre le jardin, poursuit, sans assaillir, son extension, ne cessera de paraître comme d'avoir été.

Les favorisés de l'instant n'ont pas vécu comme nous avons osé vivre, sans crainte du voilement de notre imagination, par tendresse d'imagination.

*

Our storms are essential to us. In the order of sufferings society is not inevitably at fault, for all its narrow places, its walls, their alternating collapse and restoration.

One cannot measure oneself with the image someone else adopts of us, analogy would soon get lost.

*

We shall pass from imagined death to the reeds of death lived starkly. Life, by abrasion, is distracted through us.

Death is to be found not on this side, nor on the far side. She is close by, industrious, humble.

*

I was born and grew up among contraries tangible at every moment, for all their spacious exactions and the blows they gave each other. I haunted railway stations.

Shining heart lights more than its own night. It re-erects the scarcely nimble wheat-ear.

*

Some leave poisons, others remedies. Difficult to decipher. You have to taste.

Immediate yes or no is healthy in spite of the corrections that will follow.

*

In the uppermost dwelling, no guest, no sharing: the fundamental urn. The lightning outlines the present, slashes its garden, chases, without assailing, its extension, will no more cease to appear than to have been.

The favored of the moment have not lived as we have dared live, without fear of any muffling of our imagination, through tenderness of imagination.

*

269

Nous ne sommes tués que par la vie. La mort est l'hôte. Elle délivre la maison de son enclos et la pousse à l'orée du bois.

Soleil jouvenceau, je te vois; mais là où tu n'es plus.

*

Qui croit renouvelable l'énigme, la devient. Escaladant librement l'érosion béante, tantôt lumineux, tantôt obscur, savoir sans fonder sera sa loi. Loi qu'il observera mais qui aura raison de lui; fondation dont il ne voudra pas mais qu'il mettra en œuvre.

On doit sans cesse en revenir à l'érosion. La douleur contre la perfection.[†]

*

Tout ce que nous accomplirons d'essentiel à partir d'aujourd'hui, nous l'accomplirons faute de mieux. Sans contentement ni désespoir. Pour seul soleil: le bœuf écorché de Rembrandt. Mais comment se résigner à la date et à l'odeur sur le gîte affichées, nous qui, sur l'heure, sommes intelligents jusqu'aux conséquences?

Une simplicité s'ébauche: le feu monte, la terre emprunte, la neige vole, la rixe éclate. Les dieux-dits nous délèguent un court temps leur loisir, puis nous prennent en haine de l'avoir accepté. Je vois un tigre. Il voit. Salut. Qui, là, parmi les menthes, est parvenu à naître dont toute chose, demain, se prévaudra?

[†] Ici le mur sollicité de la maison perdue de vue ne renvoie plus de mots clairvoyants.

We are killed only by life. Death is the host. Delivers the house from its fence and pushes it to the wood's edge.

Sun, lad, I see you; but where you no longer are.

*

Whoever believes the enigma renewable, becomes it. Now luminous, now dim, scaling freely the yawning erosion, to know without founding will be his law. A law he will observe, but it will get the better of him; a foundation he will have none of, but will make good.

One has to return again and again to erosion. Suffering versus perfection.[†]

*

All we accomplish from today on, we shall accomplish for want of something better. Neither contentment nor despair. Our only sun: Rembrandt's flayed ox. But how resign ourselves to the date and smell marked on the joint, we who at a crisis are intelligent even to foresight?

A simplicity is outlining itself: fire is rising, earth borrowing, snow flying, riot exploding. The godsteads delegate their leisure to us for a short while, then take against us for having accepted it. I see a tiger. He sees. 'Morning! Who, there, among the mint, has contrived to be born, to whom tomorrow every single thing will lay claim?

J.G.

[†] Here the house lost to view, its wall when hailed no longer sends back clairvoyant words.

LA NUIT TALISMANIQUE

1972

TALISMANIC NIGHT

1972

L'anneau de la Licorne

Il s'était senti bousculé et solitaire à la lisière de sa constellation qui n'était dans l'espace recuit qu'une petite ville frileuse.

A qui lui demanda: «L'avez-vous enfin rencontrée? Etes-vous enfin heureux?» il dédaigna de répondre et déchira une feuille de viorne.

La flamme sédentaire

Précipitons la rotation des astres et les lésions de l'univers. Mais pourquoi la joie et pourquoi la douleur? Lorsque nous parvenons face à la montagne frontale, surgissent minuscules, vêtus de soleil et d'eau, ceux dont nous disons qu'ils sont des dieux, expression la moins opaque de nous-mêmes.

Nous n'aurons pas à les civiliser. Nous les fêterons seulement, au plus près; leur logis étant dans une flamme, notre flamme sédentaire.

The Ring of the Unicorn[19]

He had felt jostled and lonely at the border of his con-
stellation, only a little town shivering in tempered space.

To the questioner: "Have you finally met her? Are you
happy at last?" he did not deign to reply, and tore a leaf
of guelder-rose.

M.A.C.

The Sedentary Flame

Let us hasten the stars' revolution and the lesions of the
universe. But for what reason joy, for what reason suffer-
ing? When we come to face the frontal mountain, there
emerge, garbed in sun and water, those minute beings of
whom we say that they are gods, the least opaque expres-
sion of ourselves.

We shall not have to civilize them. We shall only cele-
brate them, close by, dwelling in a flame, our sedentary
flame.

M.A.C.

---

[19] The ring or the circular fence surrounding the unicorn in the
garden, as depicted in the tapestry cycles of La Dame à la Licorne
in the Musée de Cluny of Paris and in the Metropolitan Museum's
Cloisters in New York.

275

Don hanté

On a jeté de la vitesse dans quelque chose qui ne le supportait pas. Toute révolution apportant des vœux, à l'image de notre empressement, est achevée, la destruction est en cours, par nous, hors de nous, contre nous et sans recours. Certaines fois, si nous n'avions pas la solidarité fidèle comme on a la haine fidèle, nous accosterions.

Mais du maléfice indéfiniment trié s'élève une embellie. Tourbillon qui nous pousse aux tâches ardoisières.

Eprouvante simplicité

Mon lit est un torrent aux plages desséchées. Nulle fougère n'y cherche sa patrie. Où t'es-tu glissé tendre amour?

Je suis parti pour longtemps. Je revins pour partir.

Plus loin, l'une des trois pierres du berceau de la source tarie disait ce seul mot gravé pour le passant: «Amie.»

J'inventai un sommeil et je bus sa verdeur sous l'empire de l'été.

276

Haunted Gift

They have cast speed into something that could not stand it. Every revolution bearing hope, the image of our eagerness, has been accomplished, destruction takes its course through us, outside us, against us, and without recourse. At times, if we had not true fellowship as we have true hatred, we would touch shore.

But from the evil spell indefinitely winnowed, a clearing lifts. Whirlwind urging us toward slate-quarrying tasks.

M.A.C.

A Trying Simplicity

My bed is a torrent with dried-up banks. No fern looks for its country there. Where have you hidden, my love?

I left for a long time. I came back to leave.

Farther on, one of three stones cradled in the exhausted spring spoke this single word engraved deeply for the passerby: "Friend."[18]

I invented a sleep and drank its greenness under the sway of summer.

M.A.C.

---

[18] The word is feminine, referring to the river itself as benevolent, drinkable.

La nuit s'imposant, mon premier geste fut de détruire le calendrier nœud de vipères où chaque jour abordé sautait aux yeux. La volte-face de la flamme d'une bougie m'en détourna. D'elle j'appris à me bien pencher et à me redresser en direction constante de l'horizon avoisinant mon sol, à voir de proche en proche une ombre mettre au monde une ombre par le biais d'un trait lumineux, et à la scruter. Enfin, ce dont je n'étais pas épris, qui persistait à ne pas passer, à demeurer plus que son temps, je ne le détestais plus. Mais, force intacte et clairvoyance spacieuse, c'était bien, l'aube venue, mon ouvrage solitaire qui, me séparant de mon frère jumeau, m'avait exempté de son harnais divin. Brocante dans le ciel: oppression terrestre.

To Blossom in Winter

As night asserted itself, my first task was to destroy the calendar viper knot where the start of each day sprang to sight. The about-face of a candle flame prevented me. From it I learned to stoop over and to straighten quickly in the constant line of the horizon bordering my land, to see, nearing, a shadow giving birth to a shadow through the slant of a luminous shaft, and to scrutinize it. At last, I held no longer in hatred what I had ceased to love, which persisted and would not go, staying more than its time. But, strength unaltered and spacious perspicacity at dawn's coming, my solitary work—parting me from my twin brother—had exempted me from his divine harness. Rack and rubble in the sky: earthly oppression.

M.A.C.

Refoulées par le jour, effacées de notre regard qui était leur espace fertile, les grandes interdites accourent une à une, puis en nombre, tels des comptoirs faillis en pays éloigné qui reviendraient à la vie en passant vertigineusement de leur voûte à la nôtre.

Nous nous suffisions, sous le trait de feu de midi, à construire, à souffrir, à copartager, à écouter palpiter notre révolte, nous allons maintenant souffrir, mais souffrir en sursaut, fondre sur la fête et croire durable le succès de ce soulèvement, en dépit de sa rapide extinction.

Eclats de notre jeunesse, éclats pareils à des lézards chatoyants tirés de leur sommeil anfractueux; dès lors pressés d'atteindre le voyageur fondamental dont ils demeurent solidaires.

Sleep at the Lupercales[19]

Driven back by day, obliterated from our gaze, their fertile space, the great interdicted ones come forward, severally, then in droves, as warehouses bankrupt in a faraway country which might return to life by passing dizzily from their vault to ours.

We sufficed for each other, under the shaft of midday fire, in our constructing, in our suffering, in our sharing, listening to the throb of our revolt; now we shall suffer, but suffer bolt erect, falling upon the feast and thinking the success of this uprising durable despite its rapid extinction.

Flashes of our youth, flashes like irridescent lizards snatched from their craggy slumber; henceforth hurrying to rejoin the essential traveler to whom they remain committed.

M.A.C.

[19] The Lupercalia of February 15, a celebration of fecundity rites associated with the feast of Pan (Lupercus), as killer of wolves and thus protector of sheep, follow directly on the season of the Saturnalia, a Roman festival where the roles of master and slave were interchanged.

A * * *

Tu es mon amour depuis tant d'années,
Mon vertige devant tant d'attente,
Que rien ne peut vieillir, froidir;
Même ce qui attendait notre mort,
Ou lentement sut nous combattre,
Même ce qui nous est étranger,
Et mes éclipses et mes retours.

Fermée comme un volet de buis
Une extrême chance compacte
Est notre chaîne de montagnes,
Notre comprimante splendeur.

Je dis chance, ô ma martelée;
Chacun de nous peut recevoir
La part du mystère de l'autre
Sans en répandre le secret;
Et la douleur qui vient d'ailleurs
Trouve enfin sa séparation
Dans la chair de notre unité,
Trouve enfin sa route solaire
Au centre de notre nuée
Qu'elle déchire et recommence.

Je dis chance comme je le sens.
Tu as élevé le sommet
Que devra franchir mon attente
Quand demain disparaîtra.

1950

To * * *

You've been my love so many years,
My bewilderment at so much waiting,
That not a thing can age or chill;
Even what waited for our death
Or fought against us with patient skill,
Even what's still to us a stranger,
And my eclipses and returns.

Shut, now, like a boxwood shutter
Here is a last, compact chance:
Our mountain chain,
Our compressing splendor.

I say a chance, O my hammered love;
You and I can each receive
The other's share of mystery
And never spill the secret of it;
And the suffering from elsewhere
Finds at last its separation
In the flesh of our unity;
Finds at last its solar way
At the center of our cloud,
Which it tears and begins again.

I say a chance, as I feel it is.
You have raised the mountain crest
Which my waiting will have to cross
When tomorrow disappears.

1950

J.G.

Evadé d'archipel

Orion,
Pigmenté d'infini et de soif terrestre,
N'épointant plus sa flèche à la faucille ancienne,
Les traits noircis par le fer calciné,
Le pied toujours prompt à éviter la faille,
Se plut avec nous
Et resta.

Chuchotement parmi les étoiles.

Réception d'Orion

Qui cherchez-vous brunes abeilles
Dans la lavande qui s'éveille?
Passe votre roi serviteur.
Il est aveugle et s'éparpille.
Chasseur il fuit
Les fleurs qui le poursuivent.
Il tend son arc et chaque bête brille.
Haute est sa nuit; flèches risquez vos chances.

Un météore humain a la terre pour miel.

1974

284

Escaped from the Archipelago

Orion,
Pigmented by infinity and earthly thirst,
No longer whetting his arrow on the ancient sickle,
His countenance darkened by the calcinated iron,
His foot always ready to avoid the fault,
Was content in our midst
And remained.

Whispering among the stars.

Orion's Reception

Dark bees, whom are you seeking
In the lavender awaking?
Your servant king is passing by.
Blind, he strays, dispersing.
A hunter, he flees
The flowers pursuing him.
He bends his bow and each creature shines.
High is his night; arrows take your chance.

A human meteor has the earth for honey.

1974

M.A.C.

NOTES

NOTES

N.B. The last thing we would wish is to impose an interpretation of our own on the poems, but some readers may be glad of a few notes to get them started on Char's poetic itinerary in all its richness, in which the volumes are inseparable, "every poem in a book containing the book itself." (Correspondence, October 27, 1975.)

Le Marteau sans maître dates from before the poet's experience in the French Resistance; the fact that a number of predictions of that experience recur is seen as a premonition (the preface to the second edition of 1945, placed here as introduction to those texts). In the poems, mostly brief, a lasting attitude is developed: sentiment and verbosity are pruned, the word and the perception are hardened into a crystallized unit, and a transforming oneiric inspiration is then tempered by poetic work. Thus the double current of an uncompromising *Arsenal* and of a muse "who leaves us dreaming," Artine, supply a poet's future vigor and his imagination. The dense language of the prose poems in *Abondance viendra*, such as "Migration" and "L'Eclaircie" is imbued with an alchemical lore whose attraction will endure. Finally, the short texts of *Moulin premier* further the construction of a poetics—in terse yet ample steps—as each of these islands stands alone in its statement, yet is linked with the others in a form corresponding to what the poet will later call a verbal archipelago, *La Parole en archipel*, for the overall formation underlies and links the separate islands. The concluding statement of the collection *Sur la poésie* (1936-1974) speaks for this form, for René Char's manner of perceiving and creating, and for poetry itself. "The poet causes the links of what he touches to burst asunder. He does not teach the end of linking."

During the war years, those of *Fureur et mystère*, "le Capitaine Alexandre" writes, in the fury of battle and its moments of calm, *Feuillets d'Hypnos*, these "leaves" from a war journal that is also the prose notebook of a poet. The *fureur* endures through the aftermath of the war and the Resistance, and endures still. The poet, like the man, is changed.

"We hold the ring. . . ." The preface to *Seuls demeurent* of 1938 takes up further images of linking, circular in the ring and the cycle,

289

metallic in the clasp, interwoven in the "adversary dimensions" mingling their fruits, in the criss-crossing of contraries in the August heat. Char's major poems might be said to have a "nuptial countenance," to be composed of elements joined like the couple of what he will later call "mortal partners" in their perhaps ephemeral but unforgettable meeting. They are marked by their participation in a series of successive readings, each text keeping its own profile and nevertheless extending beyond its own individual space. The cycle of Resistance poems, evocations of refusal in the face of compromise and of comradeship between partisans ("Chant du refus," "Vivre avec de tels hommes," "Carte du 8 novembre") seems to respond to several other texts, both earlier and later, centered on a rebellious adolescence and a gradual development of character, tempered in a hearth of suffering, such as "L'Absent," "L'Adolescent souffleté." The angular portrait of the central character is begun here, each poem contributing a line or the deepening of a line already sketched. It appears to us that the situation of the poem—the individual woman loved, the specific event in the poet's youth or the appearance of a particular figure in a memorable stance or a particular labor ("Louis Curel de la Sorgue")—yields only the raw beginning of these poems, each of which rapidly moves beyond this specificity toward its own place in the return upland.

Now the preface for *Le Poème pulvérisé* of 1947 shows added complications, interior and exterior. Here the poet discusses the desirability of leaving a margin between reader and poem—room, as he says, for the unknown to enter—and, as a corollary, a detachment of his own being from that of the poem, which must never resemble a typical life "made of so little respect, so little space, and burned with intolerance." Within this collection the prose poem reaches the height of complexity, particularly in "J'habite une douleur" and "Biens égaux," a complexity to which the great prose poems of 1953, such as "L'Inoffensif," and "Front de la rose," will answer in their turn. Here the generosity shown in hospitable welcome ("Seuil") and in love contrasts with the lonely stride of "L'Extravagant" and the harmony of "Le Requin et la mouette" with the anguish of "J'habite une douleur." Each of these poems is later "constrained to let itself be interrogated" by the poet's marginal gloss—resulting in a text and a commentary, this "arrière-histoire" whose distance is firmly maintained years later. "Biens égaux" displays, in fact, three levels of text: the poem was begun in 1937, after the poet's grave septicemia of 1936, then recommenced, and later, annotated.

The tragic and muted tone of "Fastes," "Allégeance," and "Madeleine à la veilleuse" situates them at the opposite end of the spectrum from the epic sweep and pace of "Le Visage nuptial." The light playing over these texts moves from an exterior seasonal one in the summer scene of "Fastes" to an interior and spiritual image of the candle in de La Tour's canvas, and finally, in "Allégeance," to an illumination furnished by the sentiment itself, rendering unnecessary any material support in the outside world: all the clarity comes from within. Much of Char's work is characterized in its most obvious presentation by shifting brilliance and obscurity, by the balance of exterior scenes and interior landscapes these poems exemplify.

The morning poems of *Les Matinaux* might appear less interior— of a more open weave and in a calmer exposure. They mark a slightly different texture in René Char's work: situated "on the temperate slope" of a mountain, whose profile is sharp ("Pyrénées") if sometimes troubled ("Montagne déchirée"). Neither the fragmentation nor the anguish of the poem as it was "pulverized" is to be felt: even the poems of love are—or seem—tranquil. A meal is prepared, quietly, like a bed ("L'Amoureuse en secret"); a grey-beige color spreads from "Grège" into the surrounding poems, where an implicit bonfire is present, as in that poem, but for the moment stifled. In "Recours au ruisseau," a dwelling for love washes away in the stream without disturbing the surface: "Joue et dors. . . ." We might see the line of cedar trees in "Les Inventeurs" as a guiding image for the whole group of poems, stable as the horizon, as the lighting of these matinal songs. But the sun shifts to the other side, halfway through: "The sun turns, lamb-faced, already the funeral mask appears."

In the poems of 1952 and 1953, opening with "the years of affliction" (*Lettera amorosa*), affection meets suffering here once more, after the matinal respite. Now the battle—verbal, moral, and physical —between opponents unnamed but present ("Le Mortel partenaire") is fought in the reflection of a primitive fire flickering over the drawings of bisons on the cavern walls, within the cycle of Lascaux poems. The texts take on a chiseled character befitting this scene: the poems of 1953 are *worked*. The contrasts remain striking, between the interior tragedy of the marginal being ("Marmonnement") and the exterior lightness of "Allégresse," where the human and natural worlds fuse in the same harmony as the previous poem of correspondence: "Le Requin et la mouette," describing the separate and yet common discovery by Matisse and Char of the shark and the seagull as intimately related. (This deep convergence of intuition between René Char and the painters who are his close companions and his lasting allies: "les alliés substantiels" and "les frères de mémoire," is seen everywhere, both in the poems and in the prose texts. Not only Matisse, but Picasso, Braque, Klee, Giacometti, Nico-

291

las de Staël, Miró, Vieira da Silva. . . .) Harmonious too, the air around the lovers in "La Chambre dans l'espace," in its celebration at once pure and corporeal. The word as a poetic "archipelago" extends from an image of affliction to an image of sunset ("Subsidence"), elevated by its grief as by its radiance.

In an upward climb (*Retour amont*) toward a lost simplicity (*Le Nu perdu*) and an interior height, there is situated a series of poems ("Venasque," "Chérir Thouzon," "Dansons aux Baronnies," "Mirage des aiguilles," "Village vertical"), whose ascent is clearly defined: from a river valley to a parched village to a mountain summit, from a physical and mental anguish to a bareness chosen and cherished. But another group of poems, whose scene is the "quarried rain" discussed in the introduction, show a landscape less obviously that of Provence. Now an inner understanding and a corresponding imagery converge in poems of a strong moral bent, informed by energy and force ("Dyne"), brutality ("Permanent invisible"), suffering ("Rémanence"), and tenderness ("Le Gaucher"). In the poems of *L'Effroi la joie* with their Pascalian resonance, the voyage is given still another perspective, preparing the way for the series of brief prose poems taking their departure from the *bories*, those ancient dwellings whose stones hold together with no mortar. The poet now leans *Contre une maison sèche*, as he did before against a *paroi*, and then departs from it. Here the architectural complexity depends on text and answering text, like two wings for a flight prepared over time, or like a problem and an elaboration which join together in searching for a way of final return.

As guardians of the present, a few poems of the past are illuminated and illustrated by the poet during *La Nuit talismanique* of his insomnia. New texts are juxtaposed with the old, creating a work on two levels, like the double moment of *Le Poème pulvérisé* and its "arrière-histoire" or marginal commentary, and of the two vertical layers in *Contre une maison sèche*. Into this night there enter also the inspiration of the early *Artine* and the candle lighting the figure of the Magdalen before her mirror, the skull a final talisman.

The Orion poems are taken from *Aromates chasseurs*, Char's most recent volume, in press at the same time as these translations. They mark the reception of all the poems upland, but never separated from the horizon of the present: "A human meteor has the earth for honey."

M.A.C.

292

Library of Congress Cataloging in Publication Data

Char, René, 1907-
    Poems of René Char.

    (The Lockert Library of poetry in translation)
    English and French.
    I. Caws, Mary Ann. II. Griffin, Jonathan. III. Title.
PQ2605.H3345A23   841'.9'12   75-30189
ISBN 0-691-06297-8
ISBN 0-691-01325-X pbk.

DATE DUE

APR 2 8 1983			
APR 1 2 1984			
JUL 2 1990			